Jesus is Lord

By Jeff York

Copyright © 2011 by Jeff York

Jesus is Lord
by Jeff York

Printed in the United States of America

ISBN 9781613796955

All rights reserved solely by the author. The author guarantees all contents are original and do not infringe upon the legal rights of any other person or work. No part of this book may be reproduced in any form without the permission of the author. The views expressed in this book are not necessarily those of the publisher.

Unless otherwise indicated, Bible quotations are taken from The New International Version of the Bible. Copyright © 1975 by Zondervan.

www.xulonpress.com

Table of Contents

Introduction vii
Chapter One: In the beginning 11
Chapter Two: Your calling and training 22
Chapter Three: Faith 37
Chapter Four: Bible Studies 48
Chapter Five: Going Out 57
Chapter Six: Mass Scale Warfare is born 65
Chapter Seven: Three short stories 76
Chapter Eight: The first time I met Satan himself 86
Chapter Nine: Good water 94
Chapter Ten: 1992 Group 100
Chapter Eleven: Billy Graham crusade 117
Chapter Twelve: Hell knocks at my door & retirement ... 124
Chapter Thirteen: Short Stories 135
Chapter Fourteen: Sermon 148
Chapter Fifteen: The future 159
Chapter Sixteen: Conclusion 166

Introduction

What if I told you that you could know God so closely and have a ministry that was so effective that it was just a normal course of business to have your prayers show up on the local, national, and international news.

Hearin, this book contains a description of a life with simple faith that put into action has created miracles on a biblical scale. The following chapters describe true stories of water parting, food multiplying, healings, and battles for souls of men so large that I've ended up in the presence of all three archangels, and so powerful at times that weather pattern changes or earth quakes would happen.

The book of I Corinthians 12:12-25 says that there are different parts of the body (spiritual giftings to be done); Verse 25, "so that there should be no division in the body, but that its parts should have equal concern for each other." So, when reading this book you think to yourself, "I don't know about that" or "I wouldn't have done it that way"; it's ok because we all have different duties to do. However, sometimes the church persecutes itself over differences that are actually made by the Lord. So, let us be mature enough to not persecute, but instead, be inspired by those differences, less we be criticizing the Lord Himself because it was by His authority that these things were done.

Although some of me wants to share these stories, other emotions say, "Why tell so many your personal and very intimate relationships with the Lord?" However, it is now the Lord's will that this book be written as a testimony to His glory and honor and that you may know Him better. Everything in this book is true to the best of my knowledge. Some smaller details like dates may be off slightly. When I think about the miracles in this book I feel like it is Jesus' testimony I'm writing about. Not so much my own, because it's His power that accomplished everything. It's just that the Lord is looking for an open vessel of faith to do them. Will that be you also? All of the miracles in the next few chapters were done in relationship with God; not for the power or any other motive.

If at any time you want to give your life to the Lord, just say this out loud: "Lord Jesus forgive me of my sins, wash me in your blood that forgives me of all my sin; come into my heart (your soul), I make you Lord and savior of my life, thank you for dying on a cross for me."

If you truly meant this, your name is written in the "Lambs book of life" so you will be going to heaven after this life. Now get into a good bible believing church to learn more about your new life in Christ. Your new life in Him is one that you will gain joy, wisdom, knowledge, true understanding of love, direction and purpose for your life.

When Adam and Eve sinned (rebelled against God) they took their life into their own hands, so their sin separated them from God and condemned them to hell then the lake of fire forever; but now we are made right to God through Jesus Christ who shed His blood for the forgiveness of our sins. In the bible it says that without the shedding of blood there is no forgiveness of sin. So Jesus being sinless made that atonement for us by dying and shedding His blood on a cross for us. Ephesians 2: 8-9 says "For it is by grace you have been saved, through faith, and this not from yourselves, it is the gift of God, not by works so that no one can boast."

Chapter One

In the beginning

What are the consequences of the fall of man, sin, and how it affects our relationship with God? Then, what do we do?

God created Adam and Eve in His own image; so we have a soul/eternal spirit and will have eternal existence in heaven or the lake of fire. God put Adam and Eve in a garden in Eden where they could have lived forever. Instead, they sinned by eating from the tree of "The knowledge of good and evil." They became spiritually dead once they sinned, then later, they also physically died (read Genesis chapters 1-3).

So, because of this, corruption entered all creation. So, if anyone says, "If God is such a loving God, how could this (bad thing) happen", it is because mankind chose it to be this way, not God.

Sin caused three major things to happen. First, sin takes away a peaceful right-standing relationship with God, thus separating, condemning us to hell, then the lake of fire for eternity. But, we are made right with Christ; Romans 5:12-21, "Therefore, just as sin entered the world through one man and death through sin, and in this way death came to all men, because all sinned – for before the law was given, sin was in the world. But, sin is not taken into account when there is no law. Nevertheless, death reigned from the time of Adam to the time of Moses, even over those who did not sin by breaking a command, as did Adam, who was a pattern of the one to come.

But the gift is not like the trespass. For if the many died by the trespass of the one man, how much more did God's grace and the gift that came by the grace of the one man, Jesus Christ, overflow to the many! Again, the gift of God is not like the result of the one man's sin: The judgment followed one sin and brought condemnation, but the gift followed many trespasses and brought justification. For if, by the trespass of the one man, death reigned through that one man, how much more will those who receive God's abundant provision of grace and the gift of righteousness reign in life through the one man, Jesus Christ. Consequently, just as the result of one act of righteousness was justification that brings life for all men, for just as through the disobedience of the one man, the many were made sinners, so also through the obedience of the one man, the many were made righteous.

The law was added so that the trespass might increase. But where sin increased, grace increased all the more, so that just as sin reigned in death, so also grace might reign through righteousness to bring eternal life through Jesus Christ our Lord."

Romans 6:23 says, "For the wages of sin is death, but the gift of God is eternal life in Christ Jesus our Lord." John 3:16-17 says, "For God so loved the world that He gave His one and only Son, that whoever believes in Him shall not perish but have eternal life. For God did not send his son into the world to condemn the world, but to save the world through Him."

Secondly, sin is deceptive. The sin nature is inherited from one generation to the next. It's constantly trying to turn you away from God, so that you would do what seems best, but this is a lie. It would actually take away what is best for you, which is God's plan for your life. Isaiah 48:17-18 says, "This is what the Lord says – your Redeemer, the Holy One of Israel: I am the Lord your God, who teaches you what is best for you, who directs you in the way you should go. If only you had paid attention to my commands, your peace would have been a river, your righteousness like the waves of the sea."

Romans 8:28, "And we know that in all things God works for the good of those who love him, who have been called according to his purpose."

Ephesians 2:10, "For we are God's workmanship, created in Christ Jesus to do good works, which God prepared in advance for us to do."

Thirdly, the sin nature has reduced mankind's spiritual abilities and perceptions. In the garden in Eden, Adam and Eve walked with God, talked with, and saw God face to face. Now because of the sin nature, mankind is less aware of what is really going on since they see Him less, sense Him less, and touch Him less. Some even deny Him since their hearts are so darkened by the sin nature they have little perception of Him, but Romans 1:20 says, "For since the creation of the world God's invisible qualities – his eternal power and divine nature – have been clearly seen, being understood from what has been made, so that men are without excuse." You also may want to read the whole context of that verse in Romans 1:18-32.

This whole book is devoted to getting back our relationship with Him with its spiritual perception so that we may receive back what was lost when sin entered the world through Adam and Eve. It's not just about giving one's life to the Lord and expecting to go to heaven when you die. He wants you to live by the Spirit.

Spiritual perception results in what is sometimes referred to as "spiritual gifts". Read I Corinthians, chapter twelve on miracles (an event outside of the normal physical realm).

Spiritual gifts for the believer are meant for revealing himself to us to know him better, to spend time with him, to help us and others.

Before Jesus made the ultimate sacrifice for our sins, he said in John 16:13-15, "But when He, the Spirit of truth, comes, He will guide you into all truth. He will not speak on His own; He will speak only what He hears, and He will tell you what is yet to come. He will bring glory to me by taking from what is mine and making known to you. All that belongs to the Father is mine. That is why I said the Spirit will take from what is mine and make it known to you." Also, John 15:15, "I no longer call you servants, because a servant does not know his master's business. Instead, I have called you friends, for everything I have learned from the Father I have made known to you."

Since we are born into sin (which causes death), we must be "born again" of the spirit, so that we can become right with God and go to heaven some day. John 3:5-7 "Jesus answered, I tell you the truth, no one can enter the kingdom of God unless he is born of water and the Spirit. Flesh gives birth to flesh, but the Spirit gives birth to Spirit. You should not be surprised at my saying 'You must be born again'".

So, if we are to know God's business (John 15:15 & John 16:12-15), then what is His business? It's everything in all creation, except practicing unholiness. With the holy fear of God I say "HOW AWESOME! THE SPIRIT OF GOD, WHO IS GOD, IS NOW LIVING IN ME!" The freedoms we have in Christ are very great!

With a childlike faith, believe in what the Word says in John 3:34, "For the one whom God has sent speaks the words of God, for God gives the Spirit without limit." And, John 14:12-14, "I tell you the truth, anyone who has faith in me will do what I have been doing. He will do even greater things than these, because I am going to the Father. And I will do whatever you ask in my name, so that the Son may bring glory to the Father. You may ask Me for anything in My name, and I will do it." So, He gives us the Spirit without limit and we will do even greater works than Jesus! The only scriptures limiting doing greater works than Jesus, is we are not a deity like him (not a god) and that we can't die like he did for the sins of the world, to redeem all mankind. Other than those two things, I can't find any scriptural reference for any limits except what might be his sovereign will in any given circumstance! No wonder we have the book of Acts. Even James 5:16-18 says, "Therefore confess your sins to each other and pray for each other so that you may be healed. The prayer of a righteous man is powerful and effective. Elijah was a man jut like us. He prayed earnestly that it would not rain, and it did not rain on land for three and a half years. Again he prayed and the heavens gave rain, and the earth produced its crops." We are being compared to Elijah!

EVERYTHING IS BEFORE US!

As a child I was told that the Bible is true, so that's what I believed. Whatever you do is what you believe in. The Bible says to be a doer of His Word and not a hearer only, (John 13:23-24; James 1:22). So, my prayers began to be in the news. I didn't know any better. His Word says that a prayer of a righteous man is powerful and effective. But, when I started to grow up in my later teenage years, I realized that my teachers had so little faith that they didn't even preach against what I was seeing the Lord do, because it was so far outside their realm of thinking that it didn't even enter their minds.

Always have a childlike faith that believes anything is possible or you will miss extraordinary things. Stop everything you are doing, quiet your soul, and just listen. Receive His peace, what is He saying, what is He doing and thinking. When you give your life back to Him, you get His; you get what He's got!

One time I talked with a pastor about Matt. 17:18-21, "Jesus rebuked the demon, and it came out of the boy, and he was healed from that moment. The disciples came to Jesus in private and asked, "Why couldn't we drive it out?"

He replied, "Because you have too little faith. I tell you the truth, if you have faith as small as a mustard seed, you can say to this mountain, 'Move from here to there' and it will move. Nothing will be impossible for you."

The pastor said to me that the mountain actually represented King Herod's authority and not a physical mountain. I believe that since he's been to Bible school and I haven't, he may be correct. However, my simple faith took that literally as being a mountain. I've seen physical things bigger than mountains move, by faith! So, inside I laughed to myself and thought, "oops, sorry God, I guess those last several hundred times those things of Biblical proportions happened I made a mistake?" No! These things happened out of God's will. The Word of God is so multifaceted that sometimes a scripture can have more than one meaning. So, both interpretations were ok.

Today many places in the world that the gospel has been for hundreds of years have grown cold to faith; they've lost connection with Christ, becoming unproductive. Besides having a shallow relationship with the Lord, it cost others their salvation because there is no power or authority in their witness.

The Spirit of God was given to all mankind almost two thousand years ago, but yet today (2011) most people still don't know the Lord. The reason is that most people who confess Jesus as Lord aren't trained fully about their spiritual gifts that would fulfill their life's mission. If they did complete that mission, the greatest purpose they could achieve would be theirs, and salvation for others would follow in their wake.

Some people can go to church and give their life to the Lord. Sometimes you must go outside of the church to get them. Some of those people may say things against you, steal, harm, and maybe try to kill you. If you know the Lord, then people that don't know him are depending upon you to share the "Good News" of what Jesus has done for them. It's the spiritual gifts that are sometimes the ONLY thing that will show them that, yes, "Jesus is Lord".

To be called a Christian means to be "Christ-like". Look at all the miracles Jesus did! About the only thing Jesus was amazed at was the lack of people's faith. Jesus did few miracles in places that had doubt. Matt. 13:58, "And he didn't do many miracles there because of their lack of faith." If the supernatural is taken away from a relationship with God, it's just doctrine taught by man. The best example for how things really are is what Jesus did and the book of Acts. In the book of Acts we see them studying the scriptures and spreading the Word with signs and wonders. We have the Holy Spirit in us! That is God Himself! When one knows the Lord well, faith becomes the normal. So, the stories in this book aren't such a stretch to believe in.

It is the spiritual realm that rules the physical realm. It is the Lord Almighty who made and rules them both. So let us pay attention and step right into eternal things.

There is no power in the name of Jeff York. Like everyone else, I've fallen short of the glory of God. Praise the Lord, all credit for everything belongs to you!

Chapter Two

Your calling and training

There just isn't anything better than finding your calling/highest purpose in life. So, what might that be?

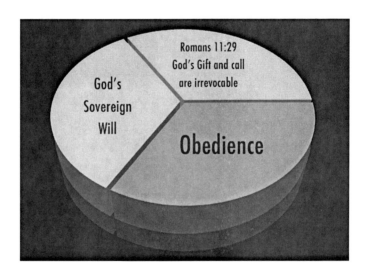

There are three parts to your gifts and calling.

One: Romans 11:29, "God's gifts and call are irrevocable." This verse also goes along with Ephesians 2:10, about us being predestined to do good works. How this works is that your personality and interests predispositions you for those good works. Since the Lord knows this, he will give work to do accordingly.

Chapter twelve of first Corinthians shows us just some of the many spiritual gifts. Just because a gift isn't specifically listed here doesn't mean it doesn't exist. There are many different gifts and ways to use them as there are jobs/careers in this world! The reason for this is that there are so many different needs He is willing to interject His blessing; His life into.

Begin to imagine discovering all that He has. Ask Him questions; Lord how would you like to meet people's needs? Do this and you will find your calling.

Don't be afraid to try different gifts. Short story: While finishing a day of hiking, the group of friends I was with began to run as fast to the car as possible. Not wanting to fall behind, I started to sprint after them. It didn't take long before one of my feet caught a tree root. For at least twenty feet I became "Superman". Fortunately, my body hit the dirt evenly so the whole thing was more of a shock than painful. One friend saw what happened, came back, and did he say….

Jeff, if you had never learned to walk, then you wouldn't have learned how to run, and then this would've never happened.

Or

Jeff! Are you alright?

No, he asked me if I was OK. Your heavenly Father wants you to be able to run with your gifts. Don't be afraid that you ~~may~~ will crash sometimes. The most important thing you need is a pure heart. The Lord will not be pleased with those who do not use their gifts. So keep seeking and the door will be open to you. Side note: be careful not to look down on/persecute/criticize other giftings. It takes a mature eye to spot what is the Lord and what isn't, and sometimes a mixture of both.

No matter what gifts you have, you are required to have what is called "the fruits of the spirit" (good character). Galatians 5:22-23, "But the fruit of the Spirit is love, joy, peace, patience, kindness, goodness, faithfulness, gentleness, and self control. Against such things there is no law."

Two: God's sovereign will.

He can do what he wants, when he wants to. Throughout the Bible we can see his timing. To work with this, the best and most important thing you can do is to know his voice. We can trust that he knows what's best for us.

Read about the need to humble ourselves and his sovereign will in Daniel chapter four.

The Lord is omnipresent (present everywhere), omnipotent (unlimited power), omniscient (infinite understanding), has made everything seen and unseen (John 1:1-5), and ruler of all (Psalm 22:27-28).

Three: Obedience.

There are two parts to obedience; keeping oneself from sin and obeying his will.

In John 14:23-24, Jesus replied, "If anyone loves me, he will obey my teaching. My Father will love him, and we will come to him and make our home with him. He who does not love me will not obey my teaching. These words you hear are not my own, they belong to the Father who sent me".

1 John 2:3-6 says, "We know that we have come to know him if we obey his commands. The man who says, "I know him but does not do what he commands is a liar, and the truth

is not in him. But if anyone obeys his Word, God's love is truly made complete in him. This is how we know we are in him. Whoever claims to live in him must walk as Jesus did.

Acts 5:32 says, "We are witness of these things, and so is the Holy Spirit, who God has given to those who obey him."

Never underestimate how important obedience is. A large part of the Old Testament (more than half of the Bible!) has to do with blessing for obedience and death for disobedience. Without obedience, whatever a person does is summed up by Jesus in these three scriptures. Matt. 16:26, "What good will it be for a man if he gains the whole world, yet forfeits his soul?" Matt. 7:24-27, "Therefore, everyone who hears these words of mine and puts them into practice is like a wise man who built his house on a rock. The rain came down, the streams rose, and the winds blew and beat against that house; yet it did not fall, because it had its foundation on the rock. But everyone who hears these words of mine and does not put them into practice is like a foolish man who built his house on the sand. The rain came down, the streams rose, and the winds blew and beat against that house, and it fell with a great crash." Also read Matt. 24:45-51 and chapter 25.

Spiritual Training

Here's my brief story that will transition into what's next for you. Growing up in Beaverton, Oregon (a suburb of Portland) in a middle-class family had all the usual accompaniments one would expect from a beautiful rain forest environment; big Douglas fir trees, lush valleys, cold rivers, big mountains and a rugged coastline. My dad took the family (mom, sister, me and him) outdoors to hike, fish, explore, vacation, camp and basically drive all over many states. It was great.

We went to church once or twice a year. When I started to see or sense spiritual things, there wasn't anyone to talk to about them.

Accepting an invitation at age ten to "Twin Rocks Friends Camp" in Rockaway Beach, Oregon the summer of 1980 was an invitation begrudgingly accepted and pressured on by parents. A few days into the summer camp, a man explained to the group of us kids the good news about what Jesus had done for us. Knowing what the man was saying was true; I and several others went to the front, knelt down on our knees and accepted him as our Lord and Savior.

Our household watched the news a lot, so, in the 1980's when hurricanes came up from the South Atlantic Ocean threatening the east coast of the United States, my faith would lock onto them and they were sent away many times. I would also know which way it would go, and decreasing or increasing its wind speeds.

It wasn't until 1986 that I attended church regularly and began getting some discipleship. No one at church could explain the few spiritual things I shared with them. After reading the New Testament all the way through, I realized that the power of Jesus' name was missing from the churches I visited or attended. This wasn't right! That's not what the Word of God says about how it's supposed to be!

One time (early 1986, approximately) at Ecola State Park (north of Cannon Beach) a friend and I were jumping from rock to rock to see how far from shore we could explore. Soon we got stuck together on one rock, because after we jumped on it, the water (Pacific Ocean) began to rise and fall; but not fall enough. The rock we had just jumped from was just a little higher than the one we were on and it was too much of a leap to get back. The water began to sweep across our rock and submerge a good portion of it. That's when I began to pray the most intense prayer of my life to date. I didn't want to end up in that cold water. After a few minutes, the water became calm around us. That calmness originated at the rock we were on and began radiating out in a perfectly circular pattern. Eventually the calmness extended about 300 feet in all directions. It was so strange to see the clear dividing line between the circular pattern verses the rest of the ocean with its waves. Then, the water slowly lowered and I was the first to spot a knob of rock just below the ledge we had originally jumped from. After jumping and making it, I encouraged my friend to jump. While he hesitated, I looked just to the right of my feet to see a six inch tall wave stay still for at least one minute! The water looked like it was bent. It was like the Father took his thumb and pressed the water down!

Though it was a stretch, my friend made it too. Then the water farthest away began to return to normal with its small waves. Eventually the rock we used to be on was totally swept over. We were saved! Amen!

Great joy and praise overcame me. It was then that the Lord opened my eyes to see (for a few hours) the beach praising God, the hills and mountains praising God, the trees, bushes, grass and the ocean praising God. Do such things, perhaps, have some kind of life that science doesn't know about yet? Jesus said during his triumphal entry into Jerusalem (Luke 19:37-40) that even the stones would cry out to praise him if the people didn't. I don't know how these things work. The best way to describe what I saw is that it looks like the object is emitting positive energy. The Lord showed me that it was praise to him. I also saw a few dead trees cursing him. This was my first time to see water part and creation praising him, and it would not be the last.

Despite all these miracles and other experiences not listed here, I just couldn't make sense of how it all fit together and why. How do I replicate these experiences? I needed help (training and teaching) with someone who knew what to make of these things. Once I realized that Christians are supposed to walk in authority like Jesus, I began to pray earnestly "Lord don't send me to share about you unless you send me with power and authority!" This went on for years until the prayer was answered in the form of an invitation to a Bible study at Leonard (Len) and Connie Gangle's rented home in Aloha (April 12, 1990).

After walking into their home and introducing myself, I sat down on a couch in the living room while everyone else was in the kitchen. There were no obvious indicators for the reputation for the miraculous this group had. There was a dog. The couch smelled like the dog. There was outdated green carpet from the 1970's. Some of it went up to the ceiling. Their conversations hinted of nothing extraordinary, and the person who invited me wasn't there. I felt uncomfortable and almost left before the meeting started. No one would have seen me slip out. Somehow I stayed. I stayed through a less than ordinary or inspiring Bible study. The thought that came to mind describing these people was "Country Bumpkin" (definition: someone who is clueless or below average). What a waste of time. But, after the short Bible study, they began to pray. The power of Jesus' name manifested into words of knowledge, wisdom, prophecy, healing (emotional and physical), etc. I found what I was looking for! I joined them, came back every week, and then became like them. These people trained me of the things of the Spirit. You will become like those you spend time with.

The most effective way to train someone about their gifts and callings is for the Lord to show the teacher in real time what is going on inside the student. Then, the teacher can explain to the student what is happening. The teacher will direct the student on developing those gifts and talents. The teacher will go out with the student sharing the love of the Lord using their gifts and talents; much like a journeyman craftsman teaching an apprentice. A good teacher will bring out the gifts and calling the student has. A student will typically have more than one teacher over their lifetime, to bring out what the Lord has given them. Proverbs 27:17 says, "As iron sharpens iron, so one man sharpens another." The student then becomes like the teacher, so the cycle continues. A mature Christian is a doer of the Word and not a hearer only. To be a mature Christian it will cost you everything you have. Matt. 13:44-46 says, "The kingdom of heaven is like treasure hidden in a field. When a man found it, he hid it again, and then in his joy went and sold all he had and bought that field. Again, the kingdom of heaven is like a merchant looking for fine pearls. When he found one of great value, he went away and sold everything he had and bought it". Just when someone thinks they've given everything to the Lord, he will sometimes gently reveal/convict us of something we're holding onto. Then, we have a choice to keep that thing that will take away his best for us, or to let it go. That's ok. When I give to him what I have, I get what he's got; and that is greatness! In Luke 9:62, Jesus replied, "No one who puts his hand to the plow and looks back is fit for the service in the kingdom of heaven." The least committed Christians are the least assured of their salvation, and this is exactly how it should be. Read what Matt. 25:14-30 says. Verse 14 says that he has entrusted you (yes you!) with his property. Will you be faithful with it?

Today, (2011), in America, there is very little discipleship that combines what the Word says with its power. It's mostly just about what it says without the power. A combination of what the Word says with its power is the only thing that will turn countries around for the better. I like meetings that have great speakers, but until one-on-one spiritual gifting discipleship happens, no country as a whole will be able to stop what the destructive sin nature does. Even if revival does come to an area, there must be spiritual discipleship. Otherwise, the people will not know what to do with their new found experiences/power.

The power of God that the Lord allows a person to have, must be kept in relationship with him. Otherwise, it gets ugly with all kinds of false motives, leading the person and the people they think they are ministering to, astray. I've seen this a few times. It's like the scripture in Matt. 7:21-23, "Not everyone who says to me, 'Lord, Lord', will enter the kingdom of heaven, but only he who does the will of my Father who is in heaven. Many will say to me on that day, Lord, Lord, did we not prophesy in your name and in your name drive out demons and perform many miracles? Then I will tell them plainly, I never knew you; away from me you evil doers!" They had faith but didn't keep in relationship with him. Besides risking hell, impure motives are dangerous. Having the Lord's anointing/power is not to be taken lightly. Would you let a six-year-old drive a car? No! It would end up badly and that's why there are laws against it. All benefits come with responsibilities.

As for the group that met at Len and Connie's house, we saw about every miracle in the Bible and others not listed as well. As the years went by, the Lord told me that what we were doing was a normal healthy restored relationship with him, the way he meant it to be. Disbelief is abnormal. The work on the cross Jesus did was to restore a right relationship with him, with all of its spiritual senses so we may know him. Without this we would be spiritually deaf, dumb, mute and blind. In other words, unable to communicate with God, WHO, IS SPIRIT. If we develop the gifts the Lord has for us, we will be effective witnesses, ready to do any good work. This you will see in the coming chapters. If we don't, it will take blessings away from many, even costing some their salvation. As for you and your gifts, just start using what you have, and ask the Lord for a teacher to help you bring out the rest.

NOTES

NOTES

Chapter Three

Faith

The best way to understand faith is to look at the Lord's attitude toward it. So what is the Lord's attitude toward faith? When a person has decided to love the Lord with all they have the Lord delights in opening up the spiritual realm with its unlimited possibilities.

When Peter walked on water with Jesus (Matt. 14:22-32), he became afraid and began to sink; so that Jesus had to grab him from sinking. So here we have the only recorded person besides Jesus walking on water, and what did Jesus say to him? "Good job", NO! He said, "You of little faith, why did you doubt?"

Many times in the gospels it says, "…and Jesus healed them all." What Jesus is telling us is that faith is normal. In Mark 5:21-43, we see that he raised a twelve-year-old girl back from the dead. But, he first kicked out the doubt/ doubters before reviving her. We see in Mark 6:1-6 that because the people had doubt, few were healed. Jesus was amazed at their lack of faith. Once again, what Jesus says about faith, and our part in it, in John 14:12-14, Jesus says, "I tell you the truth, anyone who has faith in me will do what I have been doing. He will do even greater things than these, because I am going to the Father. And I will do whatever you ask in my name, so that the Son may bring glory to the Father. You may ask me for anything in my name, and I will do it."

Now I want to share with you two short stories and then give you a trick question. Sometimes I pray for people that have a headache and they get some, or total relief. One of my friends has prayed and seen the dead raised back to life twice. So, which miracle was harder for God to do? Answer: Neither. So we can stop limiting what God would like to do by rationalizing out in our minds the difference between small or great, and what could or what should happen. If miracles depended upon human strength, then we should worry about such things. In our brain, little electrons (remember, Jesus said, faith as small as a mustard seed, those are electrons) say, "I believe", then the Lord does it. If we seek his will, then he will give us circumstances to use our faith.

The only thing you really need to know is that the Lord will provide whatever is needed to accomplish his will. We just need to seek it out.

It's just that easy. Walking by faith is so easy that most people miss it. Walking by faith gives one a sense that a heavy load has been taken away from them. When a person is faithful to God, they have a sense of purpose in their life, with peace (John 14:27). The simple definition of faith is: belief.

When you give your life to the Lord and get filled with the Holy Spirit, that is God himself (Luke 17:20-21). So, when you read the Bible, you can believe that any good thing in it may happen to you. As for me, I keep asking God for miracles, and unless he shows me it isn't his will, then I believe that it's possible.

One thing that I've noticed is that the more faithful someone is, the more exponentially effective they become. If a person is five times more faithful to the Lord than another, they aren't just five times more effective, they may be one thousand times more effective. The closer you get to God, the more avenues may open up to you and the more places you can use your faith. How many hundreds/thousands of times were people used by God in the Bible. Do you think he would find situations to use your faith if you chose to develop it? Faith is a beautiful thing to God. He won't waste it. Galatians 5:6B says, "The only thing that counts is faith expressing itself through love." How perseverant and determined are you?

A few examples of faith are found in the book of Judges. When Israel cried out to the Lord because of their oppression, the Lord was pleased to use men from their own ranks for deliverance (so he could reveal himself, use his power, partnership with, be with, etc.). God could have just hit the enemy with lightning, but he didn't. Instead he prefers to get us involved, because we who believe are called "Sons of God" (John 1:12-13). I've never seen or heard of angels leading anyone face to face in the prayer of salvation, so that leaves us to do it.

Lack of Faith

Simple definition: unbelief. What does God think? When someone resists the things of the Spirit, they are saying to God, "No, I don't want to be with you right now." Do it enough and that person is saying "Lord, I don't believe in you or want to know you." This results in blaspheming the Spirit, because it's calling God a liar. In Luke 12:8-10, Jesus said, "I tell you the truth, whoever acknowledges me before men, the Son of Man will also acknowledge him before the angels of God. But, he who disowns me before men will be disowned before the angels of God. And everyone who speaks a word against the Son of Man will be forgiven, but anyone who blasphemes against the Holy Spirit will not be forgiven." This would mean separation from God, hell, then the lake of fire. Rev. 20:11-15 says, "Then I saw a great white throne and him who was seated on it. Earth and sky fled from his presence, and there was no place for them. And I saw the dead, great and small, standing before the throne, and books were opened. Another book was opened, which was the book of life." The dead were judged according to what they had done as recorded in the books. The sea gave up the dead that were in it, and death and Hades gave up the dead that were in them, and each person was judged according to what he had done. Then death and Hades were thrown into the lake of fire. The lake of fire is the second death. If anyone's name was not found written in the book of life, he was thrown into the lake of fire'. Disbelief means (doubt); I don't believe in you.

If you have a holy fear about not wanting to commit this sin, then you most likely aren't committing it (you've given your life to the Lord, right?), if you don't care, then you're committing it.

Let's take a look at some scripture where people are resisting the Spirit, and a modern day example.

Israel, with approximately three million people, was taken out of Egypt with God's mighty hand (very long list of miracles). Eventually they kept complaining, grumbling and showing disbelief over and over. God wasn't pleased. If it wasn't for Moses intervening, God would have struck them down many times. Eventually God commanded the whole generation of men, twenty and older, would die out, not entering into their promised inheritance, (Canaan) because of this. So, disbelieving is a serious business!

Only two men, Caleb and Joshua were allowed to receive their inheritance in the promise land because they believed. More than 600,000 other men died out, (this doesn't include women and children). Read Numbers, chapter thirteen and 32:9-12. They received their inheritance because they said,

"I believe you God." If someone doesn't believe, they are calling God a liar, and will die accordingly.

Even when Jesus came in the flesh performing miracles and wonders, some ridiculed him, eventually executing him on a cross.

Jesus rebuked the teachers of the law, calling them sons of hell (Matt. 23), for they resisted the Spirit. II Timothy 3:1-4; 5 says, "But mark this: There will be terrible times in the last days. People will be lovers of themselves, lovers of money, boastful, proud, abusive, disobedient to their parents, ungrateful, unholy, without love, unforgiving, slanderous, without self-control, brutal, not lovers of the good, treacherous, rash, conceited, lovers of pleasure rather than lovers of God." Wow! Sounds like some bad people, huh? Well, check out verse 5, "having a form of godliness but denying its power. Have nothing to do with them."

If we don't live by the Spirit, then we will live by the flesh with its sin nature that causes death.

I John 3:8B says, "The reason the Son of God appeared was to destroy the devil's work."

No wonder Jesus went around healing people. He desires to give us good things. Yet, some resisted him back then and some still do today. Some churches are still debating if speaking in tongues or other spiritual things are of the Lord. Well, is it from God? If the answer is yes, and it is, then just do it. If you can't do it, keep trying and eventually you will learn to run (Reference chapter two, "superman").

One time the Lord told me to go over to an elderly couple's home next door and visit with them (I'd known them for about a year). I was reluctant (God: I don't know what to say, this is awkward, I'd rather not do it, and I could end up looking foolish here). After knocking on their door, they let me in. We talked for about 20 minutes or more. The conversation was pleasant, but I kept asking, "Lord, so why am I here?" After about ten minutes, the couple started to discuss some of his health problems. It was then that the joy of the Lord overcame me! I told them that the Lord wanted to heal him right there! Then, they said no, and that the miraculous healing stuff just occurred in the first century and that it wasn't applicable today. I discussed with them that it's for today, even seeing it for myself, and that there wasn't any scripture proving otherwise. They still weren't convinced. They were clearly resisting the Spirit. They were nice people with a form of godliness, but denying its power. Are they going to hell? Only the Lord knows. In the least, they are denying knowing him in that area of their life and not receiving a part of God they could have.

As for the person(s) who has brain-washed them, the Lord is not pleased with them! Do they read their Bibles, or just go to church and ONLY have a pastor tell them what to believe?

Whenever the Word of God is spoken, it should carry his authority (Matt. 7:28-29). It's a mark of his approval. Now, I don't demand a miracle every time the Word gets preached, but if there's no supernatural power ever, then it's just words taught by man. The bible says, 'have nothing to do with them'.

Today many who say that they are going to heaven have never read their Bible through. Not even once! Where is their hunger for righteousness?

NOTES

Jesus is Lord

NOTES

Chapter Four

Bible Studies

Ok, I know what you're thinking. It's chapter four; where are the earthquakes? We're almost there. Those type of stories start in chapter six. Since this is a narrative and teaching manual, it's necessary to start with the basics and then lead into being effective for hundreds, thousands and billions.

You never knew what might happen at Len and Connie's or Rollie and Virginia Boeckman's Bible studies (The Boechman's Bible study was at their home in Vancouver, Washington. Many of the same people went to both studies).

There would be words of knowledge (the Lord revealing a fact), words of wisdom (how to apply a word of knowledge in a tactful way), prophecy, healing of anything you can think of (emotional or physical), favor from God in other ways, casting out demons, etc. Anything having to do with life, Jesus is in it.

So, how did we know what to do? Let me coin the phrase right here, "I don't know anything, I just know someone who does." That "someone" is the Lord. When the Lord talks to someone it's usually a feeling that prompts words to come to mind so that you know what to do. Most of the time, it's not audible.

The Lord sometimes talks through a dream, a vision, or a circumstance. The more you try things by faith the more opportunities the Lord will put your way. You will also become more accurate.

All kinds of people would come to these Bible studies. Jesus always had something for everyone! It didn't matter what their need was, everything is possible for God. We didn't put limits on him, so anything could and did happen. One of the most common healings was when someone had legs that were not the same length (usually a small difference, but this caused back pain, headaches, etc). We would sit the person down, have someone else take hold of the short leg and pull it out to proper length, while asking the Lord to heal them. The Lord always healed them. It wasn't long before the foot pain, back pain, headaches, or other symptoms went away.

Another common form of healing was to use "prayer cloths". Acts 19:11-12 says, "God did extraordinary miracles through Paul, so that even handkerchiefs and aprons that had touched him were taken to the sick. Their illnesses were cured, and evil spirits left them". The "prayer cloths" our group used were generally a teddy bear, other stuffed animal toys, a piece of cloth or other object. We would pray over these things before sending them out. The recipient would be healed (physical, emotional or both).

One time a mother requested a prayer cloth for her son who was either demon possessed or heavily influenced by them. The son was in such a dark place in his life he didn't want anyone to know what was in his bedroom, so he put a padlock on it. One day he forgot to put the lock on before he left for the day. The mom got in the room and slipped the prayer cloth between the mattresses of his bed. She said nothing to him. That night he decided to get rid of all the evil things in his bedroom and gave his life to the Lord! The presence of God was enough to open his eyes.

When stepping out in faith, just start where you're at and God WILL be pleased with you. Did I and others make lots of mistakes, yes. But, perfect love drives out all fear. So loving God by serving others was more important to us than being perfect and sometimes looking foolish. In fact, while doing God's will, we sometimes looked foolish. So, let us not be like the servant in John 25:14-30, that was afraid to use what God gave him. God was so angry with him he went to hell for it.

There were several times over the years in these Bible studies that murders were prevented, because those in the study were so open to hearing and obeying the Lord. One of those times, I drove by a bar that was two buildings away from the Vancouver study. I couldn't keep my eyes off the second story of that building (this was a prompting of the Lord). After reporting to those beginning to congregate at the study that something was up with it, no one else sensed anything. A few minutes later I convinced one person to walk with me over there to ask God more about it. Both of us were now sensing that something was up. Slowly more was revealed after we got back to the house. Eventually the whole group was getting the same information from God. A young 20's age white female with long dark hair would be at that bar to have a good time, and later she would be raped and murdered by two men upstairs. It was to happen that night (just a few hundred feet away from us!) So we

Jesus is Lord

---

battled the demons that were setting up this woman for a fatal journey, prayed for the men, asked God that the same scenario wouldn't be allowed to be set up again, and for the salvation of all involved. The prayers worked and the Lord gave us peace. She wouldn't make it to the bar that night.

Another time at the same study it was revealed that a poor Chinese farmer living in a small hut with his family would be taken captive by local authorities and killed because he was witnessing. It took several minutes for all this information to be revealed to everyone in the group. In this instance, the Lord told us to pray for his protection and that the authorities would have a powerful encounter with God.

If a mountain lion came into the city of Portland, Oregon, the authorities would shoot it, because it's a cat big enough to kill a human. How much more should we resist Satan, since he is taking souls of men! In John 10:10, Jesus says, "The thief comes only to steal, kill and destroy, I have come that they may have life, and have it to the full." It wouldn't just be silly for the authorities to let mountain lions run loose unchecked, not even stupid. It would be criminal! But, look at the human toll in every country. Just watch the news and see how Satan is going unchecked. Less than one percent of the church is skilled enough to deal in these two murder examples! Do you think that the Lord is pleased? Or, do you think that he thinks it's criminal? If someone doesn't do their job, they get fired, and so it's the same with our heavenly Father. Where are the Lord's laborers that do not take their jobs seriously? Matt. 25:14-30 makes it clear what the consequences will be. If you understand fully this last paragraph and say, "Yes it is true," then your someone who is probably doing their job. If you have fear or were offended by this then wickedness has been found in you! Repent, earnestly seek him, and then go do his will and he WILL be pleased with you.

It was my intent to bring out your emotion by telling you the truth in the last paragraph. It's better to know exactly where you stand with God now, than to find out later. So, it is with care that it was done.

The power of Jesus' name is available to us since the Holy Spirit lives in us. Isaiah 53:12A says, "Therefore, I will give him a portion among the great, and he will divide the spoils with the strong." The "spoils" is the Holy Spirit. The Spirit was given two thousand years ago. Where are all of the believers that were to intervene, stopping disasters? It is the Spirit that breaks through our human weakness (sin nature) and also has power to overcome the enemy (Satan, fallen angels and demons; they are all the same thing). As we get stronger in the Lord, the enemy resists us more. Then we have two choices, back off and become weaker, or become stronger; then, receive even more resistance and get even stronger. So that's why the strong get stronger and what little the weak have will be taken away from them. In the end, this will increase the glory of those who persevere. The reward they will receive for their faithful service will last for eternity. It will never be taken away (Matt. 6:19-20).

We are to know what's going on in the heavenly realms. How awesome is that! Here are a few examples: In Matt. 18:18, Jesus says, "I tell you the truth, whatever you bind on earth will be bound in heaven, and whatever you loose on earth will be loosed in heaven." In II Kings 6:8-23 we see Elisha helping the king of Israel frustrate an enemy king by exposing the enemy king's plans. This enrages the enemy king so much that a large force is sent, that surrounds the city where Elisha is. Elisha gets out from his predicament in an amazing way. In I Kings 8:1-38 we see Micaiah observing a meeting that took place in heaven. He warned King Ahab not to go to war. Ahab did anyway and died in battle, just like Micaiah said it would happen.

We see these people and more dealing with the spiritual realm, even in heaven itself.

What army commander wouldn't want to be aware of enemy movements to counter them? Have you ever heard of a victor in a war winning by only taking a defensive position?

To do battle skillfully, we need to be aware of what is spiritually going on. Ephesians 6:10-18 says, "Finally, be strong in the Lord and in his mighty power. Put on the full armor of God so that you can take your stand against the devil's schemes. For our struggle is not against flesh and blood, but against the rulers, against the authorities, against the powers of this dark world and against the spiritual forces of evil in the heavenly realms. Therefore, put on the full armor of God, so that when the day of evil comes, you may be able to stand your ground, and after you have done everything, to stand. Stand firm then, with the belt of truth buckled around your waist, with the breastplate of righteousness in place, and with your feet fitted with the readiness that comes from the gospel of peace. In addition to all this, take up the shield of faith, with which you can extinguish all the flaming arrows of the evil one. Take the helmet of salvation and the sword of the Spirit, which is the Word of God, and pray in the Spirit on all occasions with all kinds of prayers and requests. With this in mind, be alert and always keep on praying for all the saints."

It's better to take an offensive position then to take a defensive one, only later having to react to something bad after the fact. So, quiet yourself before the Lord, be in awe, then ask him "what is going on, talk to me."

One time outside of either of these two Bible studies a prayer meeting was called at a friend's house for two people that were in the hospital. As we prayed, the Lord told me that we needed to go see one of them at the hospital right now to pray for her. After sharing this with the group, the group said, "The Lord can heal at a distance just as if we were there, so it doesn't matter." The group's statement was correct, but it wasn't the will of the Lord. She died. Weeks later, someone from the group came up to me and said, "I guess we should have gone to the hospital." So, what stopped the group from hearing what the Lord's will was, or what motive did they have in not obeying if they did hear him? The answers to these questions must be answered if we are to be successful. They came so close to getting it right. They called a meeting specifically for the purpose of prayer. They prayed (even in tongues), but yet someone that didn't have to die, did. There is no substitution for knowing the voice of the Lord.

As you will see in the coming chapters, the more skilled someone is, the more exponentially effective they become.

Chapter Five

Going Out

Both Bible studies were great, and anyone who attended for a few months felt like they had spiritually grown by decades. Eventually, I desired even more of the Lord. Desire to share the love of the Lord with others grew so intense that it was almost unbearable. The only problem was that I had no idea how to share the Lord with someone who didn't already know Him. I approached a regular in the group named Bruce, who almost every day did ministry. Lots of his ministry was on the toughest streets of Portland and at the Port of Portland. Partnering with someone who is experienced is the best way to learn. It's also pleasing to the Lord to submit and support someone else's ministry. Bruce agreed, and our first day out was on January 21, 1991, along the streets of Second and Burnside. There were things

I wasn't skilled at and there were things he wasn't skilled at. It was a perfect partnership. Bruce was a great teacher. The steps he took were simple and proper, and should be used while ministering anywhere.

The first step was to repent before each other (if needed), so that we could be used by God. The second step was to listen, "Lord, where do we go?" Bruce was never in a hurry. This helped him not to fall for false assumptions. Once we knew where to go, we prayed the full armor of God on us and dominion for coming and going, and the place of ministry. You need the full armor of God on you; otherwise, the enemy will mess with you. Demons can see in the spiritual and physical. Humans usually just see the physical. Once we adequately prayed over each other, our spiritual senses would be heightened. You want to pray for dominion. This will bring the Lord's presence to the place of ministry. When that happens it shines the light on the darkness that's keeping them back from receiving what God has for them. Without dominion, it's like talking to someone who has headphones on that's listening to what death is telling them, instead of what God is trying to tell them.

When a person unknowingly walked down the street into the presence of God, their entire thought process will change (if only they could see what we saw). It was common for us to say to someone, "Do you know the Lord?" Their response would be, "No." Then we would ask them, "Would you like to?" They would respond, "Yes, I would like to. I don't know why I haven't before. It's something I should have done a long time ago. I'm not sure why I haven't." The presence of God reveals the truth. That kind of response was common. The dominion was strong enough that it was common to see demon-possessed people more than a block away, running away from us. They didn't know why, unless they were also spiritually aware, like a witch or warlock (then things could get very interesting). When you put on the full armor of God, you are putting on offensive and defensive weapons so that you are ready to fight. If you pray for dominion, it's like knocking out the enemy cold even before you get there.

I feel so sorry for other pastors that would go out to the same tough streets of Portland without properly dealing with the spiritual realm. They would say a short prayer and be on their way to minister. They only had a very small amount of the armor of God. It was just enough anointing to make the enemy notice a slight presence of the Lord, so that it would get them in trouble. While ministering, these pastors would have to deal with people fighting around them and other various forms of chaos, because they did not take their full authority in Christ. Before Bruce and I would go out, it would take between 20 minutes to an hour before we felt a "release to go." This process can't be rushed. The first few minutes of prayer may not have felt supernatural, but eventually things got hot. By the time we got to the place of ministry, the evil principalities were removed or under control. Since the dominion of God was there, spirits of violence were not allowed to manifest. I never saw a single fight when dominion was applied properly. Besides having dominion create a safer environment, the enemy could not influence wicked, distracting lies into the heads of those being ministered to. Instead, the power of God came on them. It's the anointing that breaks the yoke of bondage. They received so many wonderful things. Also, because of His presence, many more people came to know the Lord, than with less skilled people.

One of Bruce's favorite things to do was to get a hand on someone, then have what he called "the fire" (it was the anointing) come on them. People would feel the power of God. Any time he did this over someone who had been drinking alcohol, the alcohol would leave them. He really got a laugh out of that, although some homeless people that were passed out weren't so happy when they woke up and realized the high they spent money on was gone (this also worked if they were high on drugs). By working together, both of our gifts and talents were enhanced and we got some of each other's gifts and talents.

Seeing and sensing spiritual interaction between God, angels, demons and the sin nature is amazing.

That first day out taught me a valuable lesson about taking authority in His name. After a few hours of witnessing, the Lord told me that the ministry time was over. I told Bruce, but he kept talking to someone. Minute after minute went by……. "Bruce!" A concerned feeling set in and just a microscopic amount of fear about our protection (lots of criminals and homeless in that area). It was then that one, two and then three unruly guys that were drinking walked over from one side of the street, close to where I was. That made me more uncomfortable. Then, I realized that just because ministry time was over, didn't mean God's power wasn't there to still protect us. So, with faith, I projected His presence over the area. They soon left. It was now the demonically influenced people who didn't feel comfortable. They didn't know why, but I did. I tricked myself out of faith, and learned that outward appearance doesn't change the fact that Jesus is Lord.

Those demons in them had no chance. They are subject to God. God lives in me and I'm a son of God. God said to mankind, "Subdue the earth" (Genesis 1:26-28), so in His name I have dominion.

Another valuable lesson is not to get offended if someone says or does something against you. Use it as a sign that they may not be ready to receive all that the Lord has for them, or it may be used as a tool if you keep responding back in love. A professional will always keep their emotions under control, otherwise they may begin to sin and not discern the voice of the Lord. Although uncommon, you may need to be firm with some. Just don't sin if your angry. If someone will not respond, it's the sin nature or something demonic holding them back. Don't take it personally. The Lord came to seek and save what was lost. Keep on loving them. Recognize that becoming offended, unforgiveness, fear, doubt and all other sin is just a trap; avoid it. It will take away what God has for you, which is better.

International Ships

Out on the docks of the Port of Portland for the first time was intimidating. Make one wrong move and some piece of equipment would crush you. It was night. Were the dockworkers as rough a breed as I imagined? The ships were huge, would they speak English? The Lord reassured me again and again with words of knowledge that would later come true. So Bruce, his wife Cindy and I headed up the stairs dangling over the Columbia River, into a ship from South Africa. Our first goal was to get the captain's permission to move about the ship (this was the custom of the maritime ministry). After gaining permission from the captain, the three of us walked down the narrow corridors asking the Lord for the people who were ready to receive something from Him. All the while we made sure to look down at our feet so that we didn't trip on the bulkheads. I was in front when I came across a room with two men that were smoking. There was so much smoke that it almost reached the floor. Discernment from the Lord told me that the resistance to the gospel was just as thick. So, I passed that room up ASAP. A few seconds later Bruce and Cindy went in. What was he thinking? It didn't look blessed, good or anything else but a dead end. Yet, I had to go back to join them. Note: It's standard procedure for the person not speaking to pray silently. The silent person(s) will pray that "the presence of God would come upon those being ministered to so the Lord would be revealed to them, bring angels if needed, bind up anything inside or outside of them that would keep them from knowing Him. Lord, you say that you wish that none would perish, but that all would come to everlasting life," amen.

As Bruce was talking to both men, the presence of God began to come down from the ceiling to the floor. At first both men were polite, but not receiving. After a few minutes, they were both realizing they needed Jesus. That's when the conversation became more one-on-one. Bruce kept talking to the man next to him, while I spoke to the one next to me. The Lord gave me a few words of knowledge for him. Both men gave their life to the Lord. Things can look bad, but it's amazing how God can change anyone's heart. Witnessing with authority is the key. When you witness with authority, especially with signs and wonders they will always know, "THERE IS A GOD!" And, that is Jesus.

Chapter Six

Mass Scale Warfare is Born

After seeing how effective at helping people dominion was, the thought came to mind, "If God can do that over a small area, why not a city or large area?" Even before I could finish the question in my mind, I knew that it was not only possible, but that it was God's will. What a revelation! The possibilities!

After giving some thought about going out and doing this, I was reluctant to seek the Lord for such missions (sometimes I refer to ministry as a mission, or mission from God). Reluctance came from knowing that even after street ministry, demons sometimes followed us home to mess with us (Headaches and other sicknesses. They can mess with machinery, finances, badly influence thoughts and even set up accidents). The amount of demons that we messed with for ministry were dozens to a few thousand (we generally didn't know how many).

Although I don't remember for sure when or where the first prayers over entire cities started, it may have started out unintentionally on April 15, 1991. That was the night Bruce and I got back from a trip to the Nez Perce Indian Reservation in Idaho. Bruce was mostly trying to get ministry contacts for future trips. Unfortunately, very little happened, so we mostly ended up seeing some good scenery. There were some long stretches of silence mixed in with mild disappointment on the more than eight-hour trip home. As we were about an hour away from home, we began to pray. The anointing came on us strong. Bruce started praying the anointing into cars driving around us. Some of them swerved slightly or drove slower. It was amusing and funny and I soon began to participate. I guess that's what happens when you mix power with boredom. After three days of prayer on this trip, and yielding little, it was like blowing off a little frustration. We asked the touch of the Lord people were getting would amount to something. Things began to heat up the closer we got to home. Soon bold prayers were being said over the Portland area as we drove through it from east to west, where we lived. We asked the Lord to take back the city and send armies of angels. All heaven started to break out. The weather turned into a violent thunderstorm (thunderstorms rarely happen in this area). Many angels came to make war on the enemy (Gabriel, Michael and other important ones). Near the end of our journey, a car had flipped over (it was a sign from God of the chaos that was inflicted on the enemy). It wouldn't be long before praying over large areas regularly was born out of necessity.

The first premeditated prayer over an area would happen sometime later. There were two men at church that were getting attacked heavily. They requested prayer, many people did; they got worse. Mike was beginning to have panic attacks (bouts of extreme fear that can be, but usually are not, fatal), plus various other things. The other man, Dick, was feeling worse and worse. He was turning a little grayer each week. As the situation worsened, the thought of praying over the city made total sense. Besides helping them, the presence of God would lead to at least dozens of salvations, if not hundreds or more, not including other benefits (both men lived in or around Salem; about a 45-minute drive south of Portland). Willfully planning an attack on a demonic principality, over an area that effected over a quarter-million people, with who knows how many demons, was not my idea of a good time. Quite the opposite, even though I knew it would work. What would be the consequences? I figured the enemy would find out who I was and then kill me; maybe even painfully. It took two weeks to decide that I would lay my life down for my two friends at church and for the others it would benefit. God would credit me with righteousness for this. Little did I know that these battles would grow into world-shaping events. During the time of decision, the Lord gave me Luke 10:18-19 several times, but my emotions would get the better of me. My thoughts were, "I **may** have a few weeks or months to live??" The Word says, "Jesus replied, I saw Satan fall like lightning from heaven. I have given you authority to trample on snakes and scorpions and to overcome all the power of the enemy; nothing will harm you." I didn't tell Bruce about this matter. We didn't tell either man that we were going to pray over the city. We also didn't know where they lived (except what city). In this case, not knowing exactly where they lived was ok. Power equivalent to a nuclear weapon would be going off, so we only needed to get close.

The tipping point for going out was when Mike's wife came to church alone and said that Mike was hospitalized (it was now deathly serious). Also, Dick was now dark grey and looked like death walking. I had enough! I talked Bruce into going. Mess with my friends and it is payback time! To love the Lord is to hate evil, and there's nothing more evil than demons. They come only to steal, kill and destroy. Bruce drove that night down Interstate Five while I boldly declared scripture after scripture. Vineyard worship music from "Touching the Father's Heart" series was playing out of the cassette deck, not just for us, but the heavenly host that were accompanying us. We exited into Salem on Market Street, took a left going east and basically got lost because we had no idea where we were going. That was ok, since the city got prayed over as we aimlessly meandered. We ended up in some rural area next to a large brick building that we figured was either the psychiatric hospital or the jail. Either way, it was the perfect place to park, praise God, and pray over the city that was now in the distance. We stayed at least thirty minutes praying for the city and the people in the brick building. After a time, we felt the work was done. As we left, the Lord told me what happened. More than 400,000 dead (demons of course) and counting, because the battle was still raging, almost 300,000 maimed and several hundred thousand fled. All totaled, just over one million demons affected over about one thousand square miles and many that will come to Jesus, that otherwise wouldn't; oppression, depression, many sicknesses and diseases gone or preempted (millions of dollars were saved in medical costs alone). In 1991, about $800,000 would have been considered one's lifetime earnings. So, about ten lifetimes were saved. That doesn't even count the human cost or other costs that were reduced, like crime reduction and marriages that the enemy was messing with, not ending in divorce, etc. The list keeps going on.

Both Mike and Dick attended church next Sunday. They both looked more vibrant and healthy than ever. The best defense is a good offence. There is no limit to God's power. So, why pray for protection over just your house? Why not pray over a whole city? It's just a matter of finding out what the Lord's will is. Besides speaking scriptures on spiritual warfare, also speak ones so that the people would come to know Him and be healed. Here are a few that I like:

Exodus 15:3-18
Deuteronomy 28:7-8; 7:8-9, 12-15; 30:6
I Chronicles 16:34

Psalm 18; 24:8; 33:6-11; 29:7, 11; 44:4-8; 144:1, 2, 5, 6; 124:6-8; 97:1-6; 107:8-9, 15-16; 22:8; 68:1-2; 108:13

Proverbs 2:7-8; 18:10; 27:17

Joel 2:25-26

Isaiah 9:6-7; 42:1-13; 48:16-19; 49:8-13; 52:7, 10, 15; 53; 54:11-17; 55; 60:1-5; 61

Matthew 10:1; 18:18

Jeremiah 33:3, 11; 29:11-13

Mark 16:15-20

Luke 9:1-2; 10:18-19

John 14:13

Romans 8:28, 39

II Samuel 22

Hebrews 1:3; 4:12-13

II Timothy 1:10

I John 3:8B

Ephesians 1; 2:8-9; 6:10-20

II Corinthians 10:4-5

Revelation 12:5, 7-12A; 19:11-16; 11:15-19

Write your own list. Speak them over an area; you, someone or something that you would like to have God's blessing on.

In this battle, as with other examples in this book, most of the demons die. Most people that do spiritual warfare are not as violent. For most people, I would just recommend rebuking, binding, sometimes sending them back to hell, and also asking that they not be allowed back. Then, ask the Lord to bless what was cursed.

Once a demon dies, it will reform (it does have an eternal existence). Once it's reformed, it's scared, and prefers not to go back to see if the same thing will happen. Killing them draws the attention to the chain of command so that you are asking for more of the same or even bigger battles. So, if you want to keep a lower profile (not out of fear), because it is not your style, then approach spiritual warfare with the same knowledge and zeal this book has to offer, but without making yourself as much of a target.

I've drawn some skepticism for this type of warfare, but there are many reasons it's the Lord's will. Months later I would name this type of prayer over large areas or big battles "Mass Scale Warfare" or M.S.W. for short. If you end up doing this type of warfare again and again, be connected with others (I had many) that know the Lord very well, you and they MUST be spiritually alert.

I made myself a big target on purpose as to draw as many demons to myself as possible, lifting the hand of death off others and placing it on me in the hope that they might come to know Him. This is love.

NOTES

NOTES

NOTES

Chapter Seven

Three short stories

House Bill 676, March 1991

Over a two-day period, a few people from church and others, wanted to oppose the influence of Planned Parenthood in front of a few members of the Oregon Senate on bill 676. We were like a rag tag bunch with little preparation on what we should say in front of the Senators. Planned Parenthood, who was promoting immorality for school children, was well prepared with a poll they had taken of several thousand people who they said, "proves the public wants this in our schools." They must have had over one thousand hours of work into the presentation they gave to the five (approximate) Senators. They wore suits and ties. We wore less-professional, common clothes. The public's testimony would be filmed in a room that held a few hundred people at the Capital building in Salem. As soon as the public was let into the room, I started to pray that God's presence would be there and that the truth would be revealed, made clear to all, and that all lies and deception would be seen for what they really were. "Lord, open their eyes." I prayed for more than an hour. As Planned Parenthood gave their testimony first, the presence of God had already started to fill the room. Every Senator politely dismissed all claims of Planned Parenthood! Amen! When we spoke the truth, our claims seemed valid to the Senators (though we had little preparation; an example is in Luke 12:11-12).

Later I walked the halls of the Capital building asking God and praying, "Why do politicians sometimes make such bad laws that even common people can see how foolish they are? Besides lobby money influencing them, there must be more to it." The Lord answered, "There are demons that influence the leaders here; some for more than one hundred years."

The more influence someone has over people, the more likely they will have demons assigned to them to lead them astray. So, it's important to pray for your leaders and anyone else that influences people, like the media, judges, business leaders, pastors, etc. I'm not talking about just a five-second prayer (although those are necessary too). I mean prayers that last hours, possibly having to travel for hours or days to do it. Commitment like that is what will take back our country for God. My favorite prayer for a politician is, "Lord, I ask that you would make yourself known to them and reveal yourself to them. Open their eyes so that they can see the difference between right and wrong, helping them to choose what is right. Help them to govern righteously, and if they don't, and remain obstinate, then I ask that you would move them in another direction away from any position of authority." Isaiah 9:6-7 says, "For to us a child is born, to us a son is given, and the government will be on his shoulders, and he will be called Wonderful Counselor, Mighty God, Everlasting Father, and Prince of Peace. Of the increase of his government and peace there will be no end. He will reign on David's throne and over his kingdom, establishing and upholding it with justice and righteousness from that time on and forever. The zeal of the Lord Almighty will accomplish this." "So, I thank you Lord that the government is resting on your shoulders, and I ask you to bring the right people to govern, that will accomplish this, Amen!"

Be very careful about what you say or think about anyone. It could either bless or put a curse on them. That is why Jesus said in Matthew 5:21-22, "You have heard that it was said to the people long ago, 'Do not murder, and anyone who murders will be subject to judgment.' But I tell you that anyone who is angry with his brother will be subject to judgment. Again, anyone who says to his brother, 'Raca', is answerable to the Sanhedrin. But, anyone who says, 'you fool', will be in danger of the fire of hell." So, you see that even what is in your heart may put a curse (spiritual darkness) on someone, so that they cannot see the Light of Life. And if they can not see the Light of Life how will they make good judgments?

Look around at the people you know and give it thought. What they speak is the life they have. Proverbs 18:21 says, "The tongue has the power of life and death, and those who love it will eat its fruit."

Speaking the Word

Early into my training at Len's Bible study, God told me to write out Scriptures and some personal blessings I wanted, then, speak them at least twice a day, sometimes more. I thought to myself, "I already believe Your Word,

Lord. I don't need to do that!" Nearly every day he reminded me to do this until I gave in. About five hundred words and two weeks later, I was ready. The first time I started to speak what was written, it felt unnatural and I even laughed a little bit. That immediately exposed where I really stood. I didn't believe whole-heartedly, otherwise, it would have been easy, natural and confident. I got the Lord's point right there. Many, but not all those things I spoke started to come true. It changed my life.

God spoke and it came to be. God's words contain life. I want that life. After about five months, the Lord released me to only speak it rarely, then not at all. Years later I found those papers and decided to speak it again, because it went so well the last time. The Lord said, "No." He wanted me to move on to speak other Scriptures and proclamations. After twenty years of speaking his Word, I'm convinced everyone needs to on a regular basis if you want to mature in your faith. The sin nature eats away at your discipline 24/7. Speaking the truth brings life. You will notice your confidence and outlook on life become very positive.

Anyone can say the name of Jesus, but not everyone can say it with the authority it carries. To speak it with authority you must be found in him, so that he will be found in you.

Angel Haven Mobile Home Park

There was a problem at the mobile home park that I lived in for a few years. Some kind of witch (I didn't introduce myself to ask) had lots of demons in and around her mobile home. We ended up becoming aware of each other, then trading shots with each other. She would send over demons to me, and I would send back angels, or just battle the demons.

One day after coming home from an all-day trip, the Lord opened my spiritual eyes to see four legions (approximately 16,000) of demons waiting for me. I was tired and hungry and spoke to the demons out loud, telling them they better not mess with me. They didn't listen and before long extreme pressure built up on my whole head like I was hundreds of feet under water. Then, I felt a tweak to my nose and it began to drip blood. I got out the Word and angels to finish them off. The lesson to be learned was that you must take dominion over them or they will take dominion over you. A professional doesn't let outward appearances dictate their belief. "Jesus is Lord", at all times. I never had fear at any time.

After telling Bruce about this ongoing nuisance, we decided to get some anointing oil and slowly cruise the park. You may have heard the saying "Don't get mad, get even." For a Christian this means to love people back so that they might come to Christ. As for the demons, well, it's not so pleasant. You might have also heard of the term, "drive-by-shooting", where a driver and a gunman in a car pull up, shoot, then drive off. For us it was "drive-by-prayer," much more powerful and effective. You never know what might happen until you go. We set out on a warm pleasant summer night. Bruce slowly drove up to the suspect's mobile home as we prayed. Upon stopping at it, a demon seven feet tall stuck its head around the back side of the mobile home to check us out. It gave us a big deep very audible hiss; then it hid itself behind the mobile home. We looked at each other instantly, and Bruce said, "Did you see that?" I said, "Yah, let's get him!" Without hesitation, we both got out of the car, walked closer to that corner of the mobile home and put our arms out in the direction where we wanted God's power to go, as we spoke in tongues. The power that came out of us looked (could only see with spiritual eyes) like something out of the movie "Ghost Busters," with large photon power streams and spiritual lightning. There were audible screams as it cut down about one hundred demons in that area. This was the first time we had fought partially physically manifested demons. This is unusual, because generally demons just float around like a "vapor," for lack of a better term, that can go through the air or solid objects. Once that got taken care of, we encountered more partially manifested demons in a common area overlooking the Tualatin River.

We ended up anointing two areas. The first one was near the suspect's home. I swung the small plastic bottle of anointing oil swiftly, trying to spread it over an area. That worked, but it also slipped out of my hand, hitting the ground violently. Both Bruce and I were concerned about this. It might cause property damage (collapsed drain systems had happened before elsewhere).

Later that night the ground gave way, sending an estimated five hundred dump truck loads avalanching into the river (as reported by the newspaper "The Oregonian").

The second place I anointed, God told me to anoint a storm drain. I thought "What....what....why?, a drain? It makes no sense." I gave in, doing it anyway (this is where I learned the lesson to anoint drains). God even wants to heal the land. II Chronicles 7:14 says, "If My people, who are called by my name, will humble themselves and pray and seek my face and turn from their wicked ways, then I will hear from heaven and will forgive their sin and will heal their land." Once the anointing hit the drain, there was major shaking in the spiritual realm (it looked like a major earthquake was happening). In the physical, the street pavement was rippling about one inch, like when a rock gets thrown into water and it ripples like this a few times.

When people sin, their actions curse the land. So, when the Lord's presence comes, the demons that often lie in the land must flee. This produces ground movement, like in Acts 4:29-31. I've seen ground movement from prayer so many times that I don't even know how many times it's been (over many years since 1991).

I asked the Lord about the property damage (they had to move away one mobile home), and He said, "THEY ARE RESPONSIBLE." The reason a property owner or the public is responsible, is that they will be held accountable for their sin against God. Leviticus 18 says that the people's sin had defiled the land. Verse 25 says, "Even the land was defiled; so I will punish it for its sin, and the land vomited out its inhabitants." Isaiah 24:5-6 says, "The earth is defiled by its people; they have disobeyed the laws, violated the statues and broken the everlasting covenant. Therefore a curse consumes the earth; its people must bear their guilt. Therefore, earth's inhabitants are burned up, and very few are left."

Chapter Eight

The first time I met Satan himself

You may be asking "why does he mention demons so much?" Wherever the gospel of Jesus Christ is presented, the sin nature or demons come to resist it. So, in ministry there is no getting around having to deal with it. The greater the freedoms in Christ that are preached, the more resistance there is. There is a vast demonic worldwide organization that works 24/7 to steal, kill and destroy. It's foolishness to ignore this fact. This book deals with reality as it is. Much of the world is a mess because of a lack of obedience and strategic planning.

As the missions continued, I had become very odious to the enemy. Not only were people coming to know him, but things that don't often occur against him were happening.

Satan's armies over cities were fought back, his schemes were uncovered, sometimes even before he had thought of them! How's that for counter-intelligence! Since God made everything, including something called "time", the Scriptures say, in Amos 3:7, "Surely the Sovereign Lord does nothing without revealing his plan to his servants the prophets." John 16:13 says, "But when he, the Spirit of Truth comes, he will guide you into all truth. he will not speak on his own; he will speak only what he hears and he will tell you what is yet to come." The knowledge of God was spreading rapidly and people were taught to no longer live in fear. At times the enemy was tracked down and taken out. The hunter had become the hunted.

Bruce and I had become the most feared team by Satan in the world (I won't claim, however, the most hated or effective). Actions and knowledge of this proportion was posing a serious threat to Satan's kingdom. I knew it would only be a matter of time before Satan himself would come to oppose me. On Saturday, July 6, 1991, that day came. It would be unexpected and unplanned.

Summer is the perfect time in Oregon. It's nearly the only time of the year when most people wear short-sleeved shirts without getting cold. The warm weather brings people outside. Oregon has places of world-class beauty, so hiking is the premier way to experience that beauty.

That day, Gretl and I were going to hike Olallie Butte. It's a volcanic peak that rises three thousand feet above the parking area. Heavily wooded wilderness is going in every visible direction. On a perfectly clear day, you can view fifty lakes and ponds, twelve mountains and green forest to the west that transitions into brown desert to central Oregon in the east. The final reward is a three hundred and sixty degree view at the top.

Near the top of our eight-mile round trip, we encountered a slippery snow/ice mix. Gretl had great difficulty gaining traction on it, so much so, that I offered to go back. We could hike around a lake instead. Besides, the view from climbing up over two thousand feet was already very good. She would have none of that. At the top, the view was magnificent as usual, but this time there was an unexpected bonus. Someone (or group) had made three Christian symbols, forming them by taking loose rock (just under fist size to head size) and laid them on the nearly level dirt/gravel surface. The first one was a cross of about ten feet high with a circle (or square) around it. The second one was a Christian fish symbol, ten feet long that had "Jesus" in stones in the center along the belly. The third was a cross of about fifteen feet long. This large cross was missing its right arm. I felt privileged to finish it.

I got down on my knees inside the fish and prayed. After that, I stood up with my hands up and began to pray with bold proclamations.

Spending an hour on top was enough. There would be just enough time to get back to the main paved road right at dark. Driving a few miles away from the parking area, I looked to my left to see the butte while driving slowly down the gravel road during sunset. The whole top looked like orange fire was shooting out of it, thousands of feet straight up. Was it on fire, or lava? It was spiritual fire! Many twists and turns down the road later, I got another look at it though the clear-cut logging. This time the top was a flaming red and the rest of Olallie Butte down to its base (about two or more miles across) was that same flaming orange I saw a few minutes before. The flames extended into the sky many miles. It seemed to have no end, until there was some type of cloud (spiritual cloud?) the flames went into. After driving another ten minutes, I got my last look at it and all the flames were red (it would be dark in fifteen minutes). Seconds after seeing flames for the first time, what looked like a bat, swooped over the car and screeched at us. If you've ever driven on a gravel road, you know it's noisy. I told Gretl that it must be a demon. How else could we hear it over the road noise and besides, I've never heard a small insect eating bat ever make a noise like that. Gretl was concerned. I told her we would be ok. Then, there was a few more of them screeching at us. Our spiritual eyes were opened up to realize that there were a small number, and growing, of unhappy demons that didn't want "their" mountain to be blessed in the name of the Lord. Well, I've got news for you, Satan, "Your going to have to leave, because this here creation isn't big enough for the both of us!" As the song "Satan, Bite the Dust" by Carman goes, "I'm authorized and deputized to blow you clean away." It reminds me of Psalm 18 and 68:1-2. For me, a few demons were a slight inconvenience. For Gretl, it was a fearful thing. A small battle started forming that would grow into a few hundred in the next hour. After that hour, we were going east on Hwy 121 to connect to I-205, then I-84 to the Lloyd district where Gretl had a temporary place to stay. Just before getting on I-205, I looked to my left to see what appeared to be a tornado coming out of Oregon City. It was actually about five hundred thousand demons. This group slowly closed in on us by the time we had gotten to the newly opened "Oregon Convention Center" at 777 NE Martin Luther King BLVD. Portland Oregon. As I looked up at the large crowd of demons to figure out what might be coming next, there was Satan himself. He was sitting on top of one of the glass spires of the convention center. We looked at each other, eye to eye (distance of about six hundred feet). I told Gretl not to worry and that I'd take of it. I wasn't completely sure what I was going to do. I never had any fear (the few months of large battles had already taught me well in this area), and I knew that the power of God, that was with us, was more than enough. Driving around the Lloyd district near the convention center became distracting and then frustrating. Gretl wasn't sure where her temporary residence was. We unsuccessfully drove up and down streets trying to find it. All the while I kept reassuring her that "Satan would be taken care of." I can't really blame her for a little fear. I'd only known Gretl for two and a half weeks and now we were involved in Mass Scale Warfare with Satan himself. Frustration turned to impatience, then, my anger turned into sin as I said a few cuss words. We then decided to find a phone booth (cell phones were just starting out back then and no one had a G.P.S.), and call the lady helping Gretl. It was now past 11 p.m. I hoped she would answer the phone. By the time we found a phone booth, my concentration was more on getting Gretl home than the battle. Once both of us had gotten out of the car, I looked up and around to check out the battle (a few potshots had been taken against them, so they had maintained a distance). Where were they? I turned my spiritual radar on high over the whole city; nothing! Everybody left! Satan and all the demons were gone! Satan must have overheard my reassurances to Gretl that he would be "taken care of". He took them seriously and he left, and commanded his forces to leave. Months later God told me what Satan was thinking; that he would "come back at a more opportune time." I was so disappointed! Satan himself was right there. I had the power to take him out and now he was gone. Most of this regret would last for a year, until the second time I met up with him, and did do something about it. However, there was great satisfaction in knowing that Satan himself, surrounded by a half-million demons, admitted that he could not win (Even though I was less than perfect from anger)!

The whole next week at work I couldn't stop smiling. People kept asking me, "Why are you smiling?" I couldn't tell them the truth, so I made something up. There's great satisfaction in having a ministry that is so effective that Satan himself shows up trying to stop you.

Chapter Nine

Good Water

On December 31, 1991, Bruce and I showed up to the pastor's house for a New Year's Eve party with dozens of other church members. Minutes after midnight we prayed together that the Lord would show Bruce and I what 1992 would be like. The answer came in minutes. Two different couples had different needs. By 12:30 a.m. we split up to meet those needs. Bruce went to one couple's house and I went to the other couple's house with their daughter.

The couple's house that I went to was in Vancouver, Washington. They were under constant enemy harassment in various forms, from physical (mostly headaches) to mind games. They also commented that they had bad well-water (hard water has a bad taste from the excessive minerals).

At the house, we started to discuss the issues they were dealing with. As we prayed, the anointing of God came and lit up the house. Since demons see in spirit, it was like an invitation to attack. They want to suppress anything good. So, no doubt they were getting attention from the enemy because of the presence of God in their house. They did fight back, but they needed a few adjustments to fight back more effectively.

Now it was time to teach them how to push back, not only to defend themselves, but to go on the offensive, since "the best defense is a good offense." As the principality over Vancouver started taking notice, a few dozen demons moved closer to the house. The Lord told me it would soon be hundreds, then, get much bigger. I was happy about this. My attitude was "the more the merrier." I would be glad to see the enemy over Vancover, that numbered at least in the high hundred thousand range, kiss themselves goodbye under a may-lay of spiritual lightning.

Some game shows on TV call contestants out of the audience to play a game for prizes or money. They will say, "Come on down, you're the next contestant on the (game show name here)." My version was, "Come on down Satan, You're the next contestant on, "There's Jesus Christ and there's not exactly," I think you know who is not exactly. What a demon would win is a quick trip to hell, back where it came from after its execution.

By now, Bruce and I were in multiple battles numbering in the millions or tens of millions (I don't remember if we ever hit one hundred million plus in any single battle). No! Satan, you will not oppress my friends and their daughter! I've seen so many examples of the enemy destroying, that I was more than tired of it. I had developed a voracious appetite to not only destroy the works of the devil, but to also go after him. Spiritual warfare takes lots of energy; it makes me spiritually and physically hungry. That leads to another one of my sayings, which goes like this, "Satan welcome to my barbeque. I'm so glad you've come. It just wouldn't be the same without you, because you're the main course." I'd developed some major attitude, so taking on the principality over Vancover would be my pleasure. I told the three of them the attention we were getting by a few dozen demons, and that it was growing. All three of them expressed some fear in their statements about not wanting them to come near and not wanting the battle to increase in size. So, I decided not to tell them just how big the battle could get.

Then the Lord told me not to increase the size of the battle, in fact, the attention we were getting needed to be contained. I was obedient and prayed that it would be contained. My favorite obedience/will of God's Scripture is John 5:19. Jesus gave them this answer, "I tell you the truth, the Son can do nothing by himself; he can do only what he sees his Father doing, because whatever the Father does the Son also does."

This is why I see such great success when I go on missions. I don't make anything up. I only find the will of my Father and then carry it out. There are many unmet needs, and so many believers have such limited thinking minds, that many of the bigger, imaginative, methodical or more dramatic jobs that need to be done, don't get done. My absolute main motive is to know the Lord, so I go where he goes.

If something is straight, it's straight. If something is crooked, it's crooked. When something is straight, there is only one way something can be straight. If something is crooked, it can be crooked in infinite ways. I don't want to go down some random crooked path in life. Where would it take me? It's better to try and fail, if one has a pure heart. But, I have seen too many botched jobs with impure motives. So, my zeal for slaying large amounts of the enemy would have to wait. Obedience was much more important to me. However, their response with fear about the dozens of demons was incorrect. That would be the first problem we would go over. Not only did I show no fear about the enemy, but I showed that I was happy about it and sounded off some of my sayings that you just read.

For two hours I went over story after story about the correct attitude of an overcomer; the enemy's schemes, scriptures, and what to do in various situations. After that, it was time to go room by room in the house, as needed, to deal with various issues. One of those issues was the anointing of the drains (demons were coming up out of the ground and up their pipes). Then, we went outside to anoint their well (their only water source). All this took until 6 a.m. The drive back home was about an hour away, so they let me sleep on their couch.

In the morning, during breakfast, they were smiling and told me that their water was now good; no more bitter water! Over the next few weeks, they were doing much better.

One Sunday morning, many weeks later, the man of the house was waiting for me in the parking lot before church service started. I think he was anxious and wanted to talk ASAP. The smile on his face was so big that he had to overpronunciate his words to speak clearly. The joy emanating from him was the joy of the Lord. It had very real power that could be felt. Now I was smiling like him as he described why has was so happy. The Lord opened his spiritual eyes to see many (I knew it was thousands) demons assembling in a field next to his house that would be attacking his household. He got out of his house, went over to the field and rebuked the demons, who then had to leave. I was so happy he was attacked, and so was he. It ended up in him gaining the kind of confidence that believers should have in the face of opposition. He was now free from fear! His trials had now turned to glory! He had exhibited all the trademarks of an "over-comer." He was in relationship with the Lord, when seeing in the spirit, and took the Truth to be his confidence. He hadn't just read about it; he'd lived it. This is a professionals attitude. He will never be the same.

Chapter Ten

1992 Group

Breakaway Lodge in Gearhart was by far my favorite place where Beaverton Foursquare Church had their overnight outings. Salt smell in the air gave guests an itch to walk to the beach. Each time our college-age group went (about sixty each time) the good times were always guaranteed, even if it rained on us. A long list of activities never made us bored. We would take long walks on a sandy beach finding sand dollars, a bonfire on the beach at night, sand volleyball, ping pong, foosball, basketball, making new friends, dining together, walking to local shops and restaurants, worshiping the Lord and hearing the Word preached. We even put on a short skit in the nearby city of Seaside, witnessing about what the Lord had done for them, and then going out and witnessing and praying with people. At night we stayed up into the early morning hours talking, playing games and eating way too much sugary food. When it was all over, twenty-four hours later, no one wanted to leave.

I was at that outing in April 1992, when I befriended someone who later introduced me to more of his friends. This became a group I eventually lead from May to October. Whenever I was introduced to someone new, the conversation went into all of the freedoms we have in Christ. The anointing would come upon us very strong, to the point that every man added to the group would be convicted by the Lord of physical objects or things in their heart that they needed to get rid of. They were obedient, so that they could get what he has. The Lord opened their hearts to receive a new kind of faith they had only read about. They were taught that what occurs in the Bible is normal, from reconciliation, communication and miracles. I gave them story after story, scripture after scripture about how the Lord was working those same things they read about in the Bible today.

Each one quickly began receiving spiritual gifts. I didn't know what they would receive, but then a pattern started to develop that turned into a lesson for me. Each one would receive gifts that matched their character. One man, who was empathetic towards people, developed gifts of healing, worlds of knowledge, and others. Another wanted to command dramatic things to happen in Jesus' name and to witness, so those things happened. Another wanted discernment, and received that. Another wanted to be as close to the Lord as possible. He received visions of the Lord and enrolled in Bible school to study the Word more. All of them received these things, and many more. As iron sharpens iron, so one man sharpens another. The gifts increased and spread amongst the group, so that everyone got many gifts. Whenever someone is ready and willing (also the Lord's sovereignty applies) the Lord is pleased to reveal himself. What gifts have you received to know Him better? A partnership between you and God is empowered by the Holy Spirit and will bring out the best in you. It will develop your potential, in a creative way, over time that shows you a God of order and understanding. Is there anything better than to find one's place in life? Your life's purpose is what the Lord brings out in those who serve Him.

You can read about the miracles that happened to Elijah in one sitting and be inspired, but it takes a lifetime of discipline to receive them. If you want the most God has for you, you must remain steadfast. Ask God to give you an eternal perspective. So have peace, God will bring about justice.

One of the last to join the group was Mike (a different Mike than in chapter six). Mike was someone I went to high school with and was a friend of a friend. I hadn't seen him in years, since the year we both graduated Highschool in 1988.

Members of the group said that their friend Mike was hearing voices. Everyone who heard about this was urged to pray for his deliverance. A few weeks later, a few of the guys in the group arranged for me to pray over Mike in a room at Beaverton Foursquare Church. At this time I wasn't sure if Mike had demons or not, but it seemed likely. As the four of us sat down, Mike and I did most of the talking. As Mike described his issues, the Lord opened my eyes to see that he had several demons in him. As the anointing came on me, the demons in him became agitated. The demons spoke a few times in a low guttural demonic tone through Mike. The Lord told me the demons were influencing Mike to jump out of his chair, punch me in the nose hard enough to break it, then, run for the door. I had to bind them (Matt. 18:18) again and again. After the demons spoke through Mike, I asked my newly found friends to please give me some space. They practically hit the walls on each side to get away (they weren't even in my peripheral vision. I had to look part way behind me to make sure they didn't leave too). The most important question, when casting demons out of anyone is, "Do they want them gone?" If the answer is "no," and they get cast out, they come back with even more, and the condition of that person is worse than before (Luke 11:24-26). If the answer is "yes," then proceed. Mike wanted them gone. So, he was worth the risk of a broken bloody nose (that's love, there's a cost). His deliverance took forty-five minutes before every demon was gone. He was so tired that he rolled onto the floor and couldn't get up for several minutes. We took him to a fast-food restaurant to get him some quick calories, then onto another store for orange juice. As the four of us went from place to place to refuel him, I sat in the back seat of the car with an exhausted Mike. I was already teaching him. The subject he was most interested in was spiritual warfare; even the mass scale kind. It turned out that both of us VERY CLEARLY understood what the enemy was all about, and now he had someone who could teach him "what to do about it." In one hour he had gone from wanting to break my nose to the beginnings of a lifelong friendship. We still laugh about it today and so does everyone else.

After we got the orange juice, God said to pray over, and speak proclamations and adorations over Mike. I thought, "Great." God said, "Get out of the car and do it." I thought,

"I can do that sitting here." God said, "Outside." "Why," I asked. And God said, "Outside." So, I gave in. As Mike and I stepped outside the car, a super bright rainbow was behind him. This is a sign from God, not only that he will never completely flood the earth again, but it also means that "there is peace between God and man." This was for Mike! It was a fantastic affirmation, right from the Lord! I also told him how the Lord made me get out of the car.

The next stop was to go to his place and get rid of all the Greek mythology books with their false gods and a few other things that got him into trouble in the first place. It all added up to two car trunk-loads. Mike immediately wanted to be involved in the spiritual battles I told him about. These battles were something like out of a movie, only real. How many hundreds or thousands of times can you keep getting your prayers on the news and figure out that it's not just your imagination.

Mike had more zeal than knowledge (Proverbs 19:2). He wanted to pray over a palm-reader's shop (palm-reading, tarot cards and horoscopes are all witchcraft). They are all demonic and cursed. They don't give God the glory and take the place of communicating with God. Have nothing to do with it! I told him not to do it because he was like a lobster that just molted its shell. He was getting bigger, but was still soft and vulnerable. He would need to pray in tongues and read his Bible for an undermined amount of time before even going on a low-level mission. His armor was not yet sufficiently built up. I already knew he wouldn't listen. He would learn an important lesson by making a small mistake. So, I didn't emphatically insist he not do it (unlike if it was a dangerous target). If a parent lets a child make small mistakes instead of always controlling them, that child, when they're on their own, will not discover what a mistake is until it's a big one. Then, it could be life-altering.

On the way to and from work, Mike had to walk right by the palm-reader's shop. With his newfound excitement, it proved too much of a temptation. So, one evening he called me. "Aaaahhhh….Jeff…" (In the first half-second of our conversation I already knew what he had done) "…I feel terrible…" I asked him, "Mike, did you go over and pray over the palm-readers like I told you not to?" "Yaaahhh…," he said. After reminding him that he was warned not to do that, we prayed and he felt much better, as the demons had to leave. It would be a lesson well learned. He never again significantly deviated from protocol(obedience). It also became another story we both laugh about. In a few months he would become a master himself.

The order of power is:
God
Man in Christ
Satan
Man outside of Christ
Creation
Also, holy angels are above Satan
Make sure you know where you fit in.

Within two months Mike was acting like a pro. Our mutual revelation and goal was to clear out as many demons as possible so that the Light would help people turn to God, instead of darkness influencing them. We asked God to send us out and he was willing, again and again.

"Lord, please send us out to destroy the works of the devil. Lure the enemy into a trap and save the people, because you say that you wish none would perish but that all would come to everlasting life."

During a battle, the Lord would tell us how many were coming against us. We always asked the Lord for more (I've never been turned down, not once). You might say, "You're out of your mind!" "Yes… and in the mind of Christ." Only people who know where they stand should be doing such things. When you are messing with principalities in the millions, you better know who your god is. Always remember this, "The Lord will provide any means to accomplish his work." So, fear and doubt are obsolete.

Both of us were of like-mind, as all-out war between us and God verses Satan, raged into many dozens of battles. At various times, all three archangels were involved. Some of these battles included weather-pattern changes and ground movement. Getting in the news was common (although our names never came up, and the reporters didn't know the Lord was behind these things). Whenever Mike and I got together, it usually ended up in some battle. Several went nine figures (hundreds of millions of demons slain). When a battle went nine figures, it would always span more then one continent. When putting on the full armor of God by speaking scriptures and making bold proclamations are prep time (prep – meaning preparation time) would take about one hour. Once done, we could sense our armor reaching out to about one thousand miles in every direction (most battles were ten to forty miles). That was just the armor; it doesn't include the reach of the weapons we had! There would be spiritual lightning, machine guns, I.C.B.M's (Intercontinental Ballistic Missiles. Ours were faster and took out larger areas that the regular military kind), angels, fire and anything else that seemed best at the time. The Lord was pleased to allow us creativity with the weapons we used. The more battles, the more attention the enemy gave us in trying to shut us down, which let to more battles. We needed to be alert at all times. There is no way a human can keep up with spiritual beings, so we asked the Lord to open our senses at the right times and give us alerts with the most pertinent information.

It was total dominance, the enemies fatalities spread worldwide (except maybe the continent of Antarctica). In 1992 alone, there were more than two billion. To date, (2011), about five billion slain. We were so zealous, at times in a battle, that our philosophy was, "if a demon is within two thousand miles, we should keep going." This led to battles that lasted up to twelve hours (most were about five). When a battle was done, we had a cooling-off time that lasted about twenty minutes (we would praise God, ask Him to reduce our spiritual senses to pre-battle levels, and ask God to close up the battle so that nothing unwanted would follow us back to the house). We also made sure to go before God's throne and ask that Satan not be able to accuse us, and would be denied disaster against us, because, Lord, "we are covered by Your blood and found innocent from all accusation." Affects of these battles are found throughout this book and wrapped up in the "conclusion" chapter.

The power on us was so great that anything that seemed right could be commanded to happen. Many times I have felt enough power on me to start or stop major earthquakes. In fact, all creation was shaken several times in 1992, so fulfilling Matt. 24:29, Mark 13:25 and Luke 21: 25-26 (more about this in the next chapter). No one else will ever have as much direct responsibility for slaying as many demons as myself. It is a record that keeps growing and it "will be for all time" (this means none before, during or after me). The same thing also goes for the shaking of all creation. There was more power released than everything else that mankind has ever done, or will do. This too is a record that will stand for all time. Battles like this have never occurred before. Several times, battles reached up to six continents at once.

About three separate times, in 1992 and 1993, I had a vision of the earth suspended in space (everything was in various shades of white). I visualized two large mechanical bands that went from the poles and suspended (about 150

Jesus is Lord

miles above the earth). The bands swiveled around the earth collecting demons, like a magnet to metal, then depositing them into hell. Hell was then sealed, so that they could no longer torment the human race. A faint anointing came on me to do this, but it did not last. I wanted this so badly, but it wasn't the Lord's will. This reminded me of the scripture, "the flesh is weak, but the spirit is willing" (Matt. 26:41). Except, this time the spirit wasn't willing. The gift of spiritual warfare had now been taken to its absolute maximum (any spiritual gift taken to its maximum conclusion is rarer than a bucket full of 100 carat naturally occurring diamonds). For now Satan would be allowed to continue to deceive the nations. This will change when the Lord comes back for his thousand-year reign on earth. These things, and many others not listed here will happen. One: The demons will be put in hell for that time, though mankind will still have to deal with the sin nature. Two: The knowledge of God will be common, so fulfilling Jeremiah 21:34, "No longer will a man teach his neighbor, or a man his brother, saying 'Know the Lord', because they will all know me, from the least of them to the greatest," declares the Lord. "For I will forgive their wickedness and remember their sins no more." Three: You will see children walking on water.

Yes, this is my fight, that all would come to know him. I don't want anyone to go to eternal torment. When these three signs happen, and many others, you will know that a prophet has been among you (Ezekiel 33:33).

These battles are a warning sign to Satan that his time is short.

Now look at the times. Do they not tell you that the "great commission" (Matt. 28:16-20) may already be fulfilled? Shouldn't the book of Revelation be taken seriously?

I used to be upset with God over the scripture Mark 14:20, paraphrased, "it would be better if he had not been born." How could God condemn someone like that! The Lord told me that He didn't condemn him to eternal judgment. Judas Iscariot chose that for himself. I assumed that because it was in the Bible, his condemnation couldn't be altered. Instead it was written because God already knew the future of Judas's free will choice. Even if Judas had read the scripture about himself, would he have paid attention and turned away from his sin, or would the evil he allowed to live in him deceive him from understanding it? The Lord has been watching patiently. "What have they done with my spirit that has been given them?" Are the nations faithful? The Lord says in Luke 18:8, paraphrased, "When He comes back, will he find faith on earth?" This is a warning to us. In Jeremiah, chapters 18-19 (especially 18:7-10), God says he will relent from inflicting disaster if a nation turns from its evil ways.

To the nations I say, "Shouldn't you take the book of Revelation more seriously?" It is written down for you! Or will evil deceive you like Judas?, so that you can not understand? A portion of Psalm 2 says, "Why do the nations conspire and the peoples plot in vain?" The sin nature tries to take control, taking away your potential; the best you could've had. Whenever the sin nature tries to turn me from God, I know it is trying to trick me from getting the most/best I could have. To turn away from the sin nature is to say to God, "Take back that forbidden fruit, I don't want it!"

Your life is being played out on an eternal timeline. God has not called us to have sex with someone we are not married to. This perversion leads to hell. There is ecstasy in holiness and this will last forever. Do not let riches be your god. It leads to hell. In heaven all will be so rich that they even walk on streets of gold so pure that it's clear. That's just the stuff you will be walking on! This will be forever! Don't let anxieties rule over you, for this is "doubting God", and it leads to hell. Receive the peace of the Lord. This will last forever. If the nations would start to be obedient, wouldn't the Lord be pleased to relent from the calamities in the book of Revelation? Isn't it nice of God to pre-warn us, so that we could pay attention and avoid calamity?

When someone looked into the arch of the covenant, they died. They died because the holiness of God is too great for mankind with the sin nature. On a lesser extent, if one doesn't maintain their relationship with God adequately and tries to work in God's power, the two don't mix, and that individual will develop personal problems. I've been told that some of those in the 'Azusa Street revival of 1906, in San Francisco' developed person problems. This is why. By putting your relationship with God first, do not let it feel like you are wasting your time. You're not. You are laying up treasure in heaven (Matt. 6:19-21).

After many years of being faithful to God, God told me a secret (or is it really a secret or is it already in the Bible, there for all to see, who pay attention?). He said, "If people only knew what reward they would get by doing good works, they might start doing them with impure motives, and gain no reward at all." So, now the sin nature, with its deception, covers up our full knowledge of the reward we will get, since it is done by faith. This actually increases the glory when we are obedient. Since mankind in its present form can't receive God's holiness to its full extent without dying, so too, our final reward is so great that it must be laid up for us, coming into our final inheritance only once we have received our heavenly bodies. That treasure you store up will LAST FOREVER. Consider what God says in Matt. 25:19, 21 when he says, "Well done good and faithful servant." Do you realize the consequences of this? Jesus said, "Heaven and earth will pass away, but my words will never pass away" (Matt. 24:35). So God spoke and creation was made (Genesis 1)! How awesome is that! A creation so big that even our biggest telescopes, looking out billions of light years away, cannot see the end of it. However, Jesus said, "Heaven and earth will disappear." Now even modern science has figured out that the universe will collapse in on itself and be no more in about one hundred trillion years. So, God spoke something as great as creation into existence, but it will pass away. Yet to all those who are faithful, He says, "Well done good and faithful servant." What kind of mark does that put on your life? That will last forever! Can you possibly comprehend what kind of life that will bring you? You're going to receive something more valuable than all creation! I Corinthians 2:9 says, "However, as it is written:

No eye has seen, no ear has heard, no mind has conceived what God has prepared for those who love him – but God has revealed it to us by His Spirit." You are more valuable than creation. You have an eternal spirit that will not pass away. Let us live our lives in such a way that we show trust in God, not as worldly minded people who's only reward is in this life. Since their reward is temporary they must use temporary means (evil) to get what they want. Then those temporary things pass away.

One time I asked the Lord what he was thinking. My mind was too small to be given a full answer. There was a ten-second pause before he answered. He said that he knew where every atom was and is and will be in the future forever, including the quarks that make up those atoms, and so forth. He even created something called, "time." No wonder prophecy is so easy for Him to fulfill. To Him it isn't. His statement to me confirms John 1:1-3 (that all things were created by Him, and for Him). I am in awe. There isn't anything greater we can put our trust in. The reason Jesus told the story of Lazarus, the beggar, (Luke 16:19-31) was to give us hope that no matter what happens in this life, we should remain faithful. He will justify us. If you haven't already given your life to the Lord, go back to the introduction and pray the prayer of salvation.

Chapter Eleven

Billy Graham Crusade

When I heard that the famous evangelist Billy Graham was coming to town in early September 1992, to Portland, Oregon, it was the best possible news. After more than one year of M.S.W., it seemed like the perfect culmination for large amounts of people to hear the Word and give their lives to Jesus. The free multi-day, multi-sermon event was well organized and advertised. Churches throughout the area were encouraged to participate. Volunteers in the hundreds, perhaps thousands, came to perform various tasks including counseling people who would come forward to receive Jesus as their savior.

All over the Portland area signs were in people's yards proclaiming the event. It was an exciting time. Would a revival break out that so many, including Mike and I, were praying for? When people prayed for a city, the Lord heard their requests and sent us out.

Even months before the crusade, there were a few battles for it. One of those ended up with millions of angels coming out from the gates of heaven like a waterfall. Those angels slew millions of demons as they swept through the area at near supersonic speed. In the spiritual realm, much of the city was consumed by holy fire.

Although the Lord never specifically pinpointed who was casting curses and witchcraft against the crusade, we were running into professional grade resistance from witches, warlocks and the like. Why would anyone do such horrible things? I have no idea. Not only are their weapons a lot less powerful and interesting than the Lord's, they will also have to pay with their souls for it. So, if you're one of those, take my advice; it isn't worth whatever you thought you could get out of it.

The day before (or the day before that, I'm not sure) the crusade, the final battle for it would take place. I would drive with Mike in a large loop from Beaverton, Highway 217, I-5 South, east on I-205, turning into I-5 at Vancover Washington, turn south on I-5, then into Portland to the Civic Stadium, where the crusade would take place.

Before the night of the final battle, I sensed that Satan himself might show up. So, I asked the Lord for it to happen. If it was to happen, it would give me the perfect opportunity to make up for letting Satan slip through my grip, unscathed just over one year before. The more people pray for a city, the more those prayers accumulate. Little did we know that once those prayers were released it would become the world's largest battle between two or more believers (still a record as of 2011).

I can feel the level of prayer over an area during a battle; the more prayer, the more release of power. The people in the area were praying for this event more than any other to date.

Less than two hours into the eight-hour battle, things started heating up with I.C.B.M.'s going global (mostly North America, then Asia). Just before Oregon City, an idea popped into my head, "wouldn't it be awesome if an angel was in an F-15 fighter jet." I spoke it into being. The angel in the jet descended near us at a high speed with its machine guns and missiles firing, taking out demons. It quickly ran out of ammunition. I prayed that it would have unlimited ammunition, and so it was. It was taking out square miles of demons, quickly. Then I thought, "What does a fighter jet need; an Aircraft carrier;" and, that happened. Then a battleship and more jets were added. The level of creativity of weaponry would be more diverse than any other battle I've been in. It was all due to the high level of prayers for this event. We were aware that Satan himself wasn't in the area. We asked God to change that. About the time we passed the city of Clackamas, a stronger than average demon left the area to alert Satan of this huge battle. The message from the demon would lure Satan to the battle. We tracked the demon across the globe to Europe, where Satan was (in or near Germany). Then Satan came, streaking back across the globe, at about twice the rate of speed of the messenger demon. All of this took about one hour and ten minutes, before Satan was near us. I bound Satan with chains and ropes in Jesus' name, then bound him to the hood of my car as a hood ornament. By now we were already headed south along I-5. Satan was bound in Vancover, Washington about ten miles north of the Oregon border. The carrier fleet turned north with us up I-205, then kept going to Seattle, British Columbia, Yukon and that area, and Alaska. It might have reached Russia before disappearing. As the casualties mounted over six hundred million, the thought came to mind, "Could we hit the one billion mark!?" That encouraged us to try that much harder. However, I think it might have gone up to maybe eight hundred million.

What the Lord has is so awesome! I can hardly wait to see the re-runs of this and other battles when I get to heaven. I know those angels that got to participate will be thanking me for the ride of their lives.

When we crossed the I-5 bridge over the Columbia River, the "Welcome to Oregon" sign made us laugh hysterically, because Satan had to helplessly watch the defeat of the armies from the hood of my car.

As we came near downtown Portland, I needed to concentrate more on my driving to make sure I got the right exit to Civic Stadium, so we roughed up Satan and sent him to hell.

Before walking around Civic Stadium (it's now called PGE Park, at S.W. Morrison St and 18th Ave.) we prayed over Lincoln Field at Lincoln High School. This was the overflow area (the stadium wasn't big enough).

Minutes after getting onto Lincoln Field, we looked up to see clouds coming in as the wind whipped around us. This side effect was from the battle. Next, we walked around Civic Stadium. The prayers over these areas took around an hour. Someone had freshly taken bumper stickers (3" x 10") and put them on several stadium exit doors. They read, "My name is Legion" in black and white. Someone wasn't happy about the crusade.

Our next stop was the parking lot of Beaverton Foursquare Church. As we were taking time to wrap up the mission and see if we could get up to one billion slain, I looked up at the stars to see that all creation was shaking! The shaking looked similar to the shaking I saw in Angel Haven Mobile Home Park in 1991, when that small local earthquake happened. I also saw all the stars praising God! It looked similar to when I saw many things at the beach praising God. I think this was the first time I saw either of those two things happen.

The citywide revival that many were hoping for, including us, never materialized. My mom did give her life to the Lord at one of the meetings. It would take her a few more years though to realize that "nice people don't go to heaven." You're saved by God's grace and accepted through faith that Jesus has died for your sins. So, there was some personal victory in it for me besides the glorious battle.

Our usual custom after wrapping up a battle was to get something to eat with protein in it. Battles lasting a whole work day were intense and made us hungry.

In a different battle on December 12, 1992, I also saw all creation shake and praise God. That battle went into the hundreds of millions, over more than one continent. The Lord opened our eyes to also see that a witch had skillfully set curses over a huge area in and around Portland for hundreds of square miles, and many miles high. She was very good, in a bad way, at what she did. We prayed against and dissolved those curses. The curses looked like individual stacked blocks of about one cubic mile each.

Chapter Twelve

Hell knocks at my door and Retirement

In early 1993, a few members of Len's Thursday night Bible study told of constant demonic harassment that was fairly serious. I knew it wasn't going to stop. They were targeted.

Though they were more friends of friends, I asked a few questions and told them that I dealt in these kinds of situations and would help. It was immediately clear that intervention was God's will. Going and praying over the city had the Bible study's full support. Whenever I prayed over an area, the people there always got immediate relief.

While considering logistics of the mission, God told me that I wouldn't be going on it with anyone else. This didn't make me happy at all! When doing big spiritual things like this, it isn't just more fun with someone else, it's easier to see in the spirit because of "iron sharpening iron." The Lord puts you in the same mindset and shows each person similar things so that they can work together. A mission is usually more effective with two or more people. After weeks of negotiation, God wouldn't change his mind. I even said to him, "ok, if you want me to go alone, as a confirmation, I would like you to help me buy a Rolls Royce, or have someone give me one" (This is my favorite car). Unfortunately, that didn't happen. I told the couple that I would go down there and take care of business Friday, March 26, 1993. I didn't know at the time, but the City of Lebanon, Oregon is a sensitive spot that Satan didn't want messed with! The two times I've personally prayed over it, major consequences happened. This would be the first time.

In February and March of 1993, there were lots of battles. The enemy was putting serious pressure on me and I was fighting back hard. The day before the battle in Lebanon, an earthquake of magnitude 5.6 on the Richter scale woke me up at 5:43 a.m. The walls were shaking back and forth pretty good in my apartment. It was a shot across the bow from the enemy saying, "Don't go to Lebanon," and "I'm closing in on you." The quake caused only minor damage mostly around its epicenter of the city Scotts Mills (about thirty miles from my apartment in Tualatin). The media would name it "the spring break quake" since it happened during the school children's spring break. The whole episode, along with some kind of battle, nearly every other day for the last six weeks, left me still questioning if going by myself, overnight, out of town, about two hours away from home, was a good idea. Nevertheless, it was God's will. So the next day on that Friday afternoon I drove south to Salem. At the Market Street exit in Salem, and with the hotel I would be staying at in my sights, there was a spectacular full-size Rolls Royce at the intersection I was about to go through. It was just the kind of car I wouldn't mind owning! Inside, a cute young woman my age was driving it! She smiled at me as we went in opposite directions. For a single, twenty-two year old man wanting a girl and a car like that, it was like God was teasing me! I would have rather been in that car with her, then slaying demons. Rolls Royces are uncommon in Oregon. I've never seen anyone else driving one in Salem. Two years later in 1995, God helped me buy a 1977 Rolls Royce Silver Wraith II, and afford it to, even though I was only making about half the average American wage.

I prayed that the hotel would give me the perfect room to stay in and they did. It was on the top floor facing south toward Lebanon.

The prep time started at 7 p.m. and went really well. I commanded and saw a bubble of light over the city. It was about fifteen miles in diameter and had the same arc as a rainbow. The next step was to drive almost one more hour south and pray over the small town. The closer I got, the less anointing I felt. By the time I went through and out of town on the other side, I felt the opposite of anointing. It seemed like a waste of time. It was depressing and a real let down, but I knew that it was his will, so I kept going. Everything finished up back at the hotel at midnight.

On Sunday, March 28, I started to find out just how much Satan didn't want Lebanon prayed over and just how tired he was of me. At 11 p.m. my spiritual eyes honed in on a huge demon staring at me. He just looked to observe only, partly out of fear and respect for me, and partly because he wanted to gather information on me. At that time, I chose not to mess with him either. I was more interested in finding out why he was in town. After some consideration, I estimated that he was between Satan's NO.3 to NO.6 right-hand man. He would be in charge of whatever it was that they were up to. So, whatever they were planning, it must be serious. Satan himself dare not show up, and never did show up, less he be detected. He was very much afraid, so he sent others. It would take about one month to figure out what they were planning.

After meeting Satan himself twice in battle over two years, with dozens of big battles which he kept losing, he was more than just a little tired of me. This time his plan was not only to take me out if possible, but to inflict major damage on the metro area I called home. He wanted revenge bad. He wanted to stop the powerful ministry that was spreading everywhere the knowledge of God, with our freedoms in Christ. This ultimate retribution would turn into the largest battle (up to 2011) ever, between one person and Satan.

Enemy scouts came into Portland to check the fault line that goes in a crooked north/south line along the Willamete and Columbia Rivers. They were checking it for tension in the rocks for a possible earthquake. Demons are supernatural beings that can detect forces in nature to enhance or create disasters (like fault lines for earthquakes, or warm ocean water for hurricanes, etc. The more cursed a land is, the easier it is for them to create a disaster). Apparently, they found what they were looking for. Satan himself pulled away most of his forces that were creating hurricanes along the east coast of the United States (the forces that carried out the last two years of them, 1991 and 1992) then sent them my way. In 1992, hurricane Andrew hit the U.S. It was the country's worst ever, natural disaster up to that point (total losses would be equal to about forty thousand lifetimes worth of work/ tens of billions of dollars and effecting millions of lives). The storm was about three hundred miles across, with winds up to 175 mph. This is the force I would be dealing with.

Into April and early May, some of the Thursday night Bible study members were sensing something coming. By mid May we all knew it would be a major earthquake.

In early May, Satan's forces numbering almost a half billion, took a few days to cross the country and settle in an encampment twenty miles from me. That place was under the Columbia River, in and around Troutdale. As they crossed the country, they spawned small disasters on the way. By the time they were crossing through Montana, the column of them was over one hundred miles long north to south, by about ten miles wide. Over about one week, the demons would link up like a chain-link fence in the fault line. Once that was completed, they would partially physically manifest as much as the rock would allow, then start shaking to produce what would be a magnitude 7.1 earthquake (approx 7.1).

A few days before the quake, some of the Thursday night Bible study were gathering emergency supplies for it (including Len and Connie).

Two weeks before the quake, I started asking the Lord about stopping it by wiping out the enemy. He did not release me to go. Over and over, more than fifty times over, I asked what person should accompany me to the battle. The Lord chose no one. My family, friends and myself could be harmed or die. What about my job and the financial impact? Was it the Lord's will that this happen? The city had done much evil. "Lord, anything you want I'll do. My life, and the lives of all I know, and the city is in your hands." The only thing the Lord allowed me to do was to zero in on the head demon and take him out (a few days before the quake).

The Lord remained silent until just hours before the quake (I think it was going to take place early a.m., May 19, 1993). Minutes before going to bed on May 18, the Lord said, "Praise me." So I did. The apprehension of the situation quickly fell off of me and the worship became pleasurable. Only a few minutes into worship, the power of God came very strongly. It radiated from my head down to my feet, back and forth. The Lord wanted the power released almost as soon as it came on me, but I delayed slightly. Once I did release the power, it shot out of my body, down my arms and both my hands, which were together and pointed towards Portland. It came out as a single missile of light that took one second to reach the ground under Portland, where it exploded, vaporizing the enemy! The city was saved!!!! It was saved!!!

The blow dealt to Satan was so great, that for the next two years (1993 and 1994) the hurricanes along the east coast were significantly less destructive than some years before or after.

Under some circumstances, spiritual light is seen with the physical eye. The explosion was so big, that it could easily be seen from space, if the Lord allowed it. I wonder if N.A.S.A. or anyone else may have a picture of unexplained light expanding rapidly around 11 p.m., or, for that matter, any other battle.

Because I delayed releasing the power, not one hundred percent of the demons died that were supposed to, some on the very fringes, greater than the diameter of the explosion, (approximately twenty miles in diameter) lived. A few days later, before they moved on, they created a very small earthquake at their original encampment under the Columbia River by Troutdale, as a last harrah, as if to say, "Yah, we're still here."

The whole thing was like something out of the book of Judges, where the people cried out to God (from the east coast) for deliverance from their oppression (hurricanes). God found and sent a willing deliverer that would go in his name, and his name alone to deliver them. As for the enemy, he was led right into a trap.

PRAISE YOU LORD!

Retirement

After two years of Mass Scale Warfare, I needed a rest from it. I asked the Lord for at least a several-year rest with no exact restart date. A person on this intense of a level can only take so much. I don't think there is anything I would trade those moments for, but I needed a rest. God granted my request.

I also think that Satan was ready to back off, because he kept losing. It took two years and about three billion of his forces to be slain, for him to figure that one out. If it was me,

I think I would have caught on a little faster. I guess that's what happens when you are deceived. I am so glad that I am on the winning side!

There would be no regular long list of battles until 2006, when the Lord had me train someone new. So, for thirteen years there would only be a few big battles.

I knew the work needed to continue, so I asked the Lord several times to give at least some of my mantle to someone else, at least for a time. I didn't feel a leading on whom it should go to. I found out later who the Lord chose. It was someone from church that I'd known for a few years. As she described various prayer events in her life, I knew it was her. One of those times she described rebuking a large principality out of the ground from a certain country. Shortly later, that country had a large earthquake that killed many people. She thought that she had something to do with the earthquake, and she was right. But, I didn't tell her that. I wasn't sure what to say to her because she was distressed about it. My experience taught me that when large amounts of demons come out of the ground, there can be movement.

I asked the Lord about it and he said, "THEY ARE RESPONSIBLE," meaning the people of the county. It was the same answer God gave me about the damage to Angel

Haven Mobile Home Park. The people will be held accountable for having a cursed land that their own sins created. She was not only completely innocent in the Lord's eyes, but she had been obedient in rebuking that principality.

"Lord, let your light push away darkness (that principality) that the people may come to know you. Amen."

Chapter Thirteen

Short Stories

Violence

Ask the Lord to send you out to bind up spirits that don't belong there. He is willing.

The Lord sent me, and someone else, out to a spot in inner East Portland (June 10, 2006). It was an area known for crime. The longest portion of prayer was rebuking and binding the spirit of violence. Months later, the news reported that in the second half of the year, the murder rate had dramatically gone down. So much so, that many officers could now be assigned to cold cases of old unsolved murders. I don't know about you, but a few hours of time seem worth the ten or more lives that didn't get taken away. That doesn't even include all the other chaos or crimes that didn't happen.

In late 2009, another person and I were assigned by the Lord to pray in a similar fashion for Dallas, Texas. After several prayers, each over several months, we felt that whatever work was assigned to us, was done. In early 2011, I saw an article on the internet that the murder rate for Dallas in 2010 was the lowest since 1967, at 147. The article gave credit to better policing and medical care. The Lord did use those things, but once again, nothing of the Lord's hand being in it was mentioned. About two dozen didn't die, that would have died. Question: what about the 147 that did die? Answer: The Lord only allowed us to go so far. The people living there have to figure it out. They have their own free will.

Examples like these are common for me. If a certain type of crime in a certain place bothered me, I would get the unction to pray against it, and whatever it was would make a noticeable decrease.

Oregon, Hwy 30, August 20, 2006

The Lord sent me, and someone else, to pray over Northwest Portland, then up to Rainer along Hwy 30. I was aware that one person, maybe two, would be drowned along this area that weekend or the next (probably in the Columbia

River). The prayers went really well. The majority of the anointing stretched over this area. As I watched the news that night, they had nothing bad to say about the areas that got prayed over. Areas on the east side of Portland, that didn't get prayed over, had the usual bad things happen.

Beaverton, Oregon City Hall

One day God said, "Go pray over Beaverton City Hall" (about 2003?). I thought "Great, our leaders need it. They could use some prayer that the Lord would direct them, and that demons trying to influence them would be kicked out of the building." After parking in their lot, I prayed while still in my car, facing the front of the building. Things were going well with many of the customary Bible verses I was used to speaking. The Lord said to pray for the police. That prayer went on and on. I thought, "Lord, nothing happens in Beaverton, maybe a few drunk drivers, or people speeding through a red light!" The Lord knows best, so praying just for them took about twenty minutes. Most of that was for their safety. What was going on?

A few weeks later the news reported a police shooting in Beaverton! The news said that two officers wanted to pull over a known felon for a traffic ticket, but he got to his house and shut the door behind him. The two police officers went to his door where they thought they heard a scream coming from the inside. So, they entered the house without a search warrant. The felon shot at them from close range, as both officers tried to get in. The felon lost his life, but both officers were unhurt. The Lord told me "one dead one wounded" (meaning one officer would die and the other would be wounded). "Ok, God, now I understand."

Was two hours of my time worth it to keep an officer from dying and the other being badly wounded? Yes! But, it didn't actually take two hours of my time. It's taken a lifetime of faithfulness in seeking after God. I wish more people who call themselves believers in the Lord would feel the same way as I do. There would be almost zero crime.

Since that day, many years ago, Beaverton has allowed the number of immoral businesses to increase within its borders. It has at least one or more of these businesses: porn store, topless bar, a psychic and others. Increasingly, they are turning away from God's blessings. The next time a shooting occurs someday, will the Lord send me out? Will anyone in the police department pay attention and hear the voice of the Lord? They are steadily decreasing that possibility. Did the news program see the angels and the Lord help the officers? God was given no credit! They saw nothing and they knew nothing! How separated from God, man has become.

Two Parenting Stories

I know a nice Christian couple that go to church regularly. They pray, they don't cuss, and sometimes they help strangers. They brought a son up in church, but that son isn't following the Lord. What happened? The anointing of God wasn't in their midst, so their son never got that powerful revelation that Jesus is his Savior. At least one issue that was holding the anointing back, that I became aware of, was the man of the house had some pornography. Sin and God don't mix. So, why should the Spirit of God be with that household? Having sin in one's life is a dangerous game. How much it will hurt that person sinning or someone else is a gamble. As far as I know, their son is still alive. I hope and pray he figures it out before he steps into eternity. Was that porn, or anything else in their heart that they may have held back from the Lord, that stopped them from the kind of faith that would have revealed that Jesus is Lord to their son, worth it?

You might think that what I am saying is harsh, but the consequences of not telling the truth are even harsher. I care about you, so I will take the risk of offending you.

In another parenting story, the opposite took place. There was a very anointed couple of God, who saw miracles all the time. I enjoy hearing their stories, and respect them very much. However, the husband told me that all of his children used to, but no longer, follow the Lord. Why? He said that every day he would pray blessings of God on them. Since a prayer of a righteous man is powerful and effective, that's what his children got. Sounds good, right?

Here's an analogy that shows why this wasn't the best thing to do in this situation. And I stress, "this situation." No two situations are absolutely the same. So, I say it again, "the most important thing is to know the voice of the Lord."

Analogy: If an ordinary working person was given ten-days wages to them without working for it, day after day, year after year, what would that person do?... They wouldn't need to work for the blessings of God anymore. Praying for someone helps them out, but eventually they have to want it themselves. There are no grandchildren of God.

Five things to pray for

We are responsible to pray for anyone who would have influence over others (remember chapter seven, "house bill 676") and how demons were influencing lawmakers for more than one hundred years). Right now the ones that hold the most influence are the media. Most of the media today are leading people into all kinds of wickedness. Call a meeting of people and ask God for wisdom regarding effective prayers and what other action you can take.

In 2007, the Lord gave me a list of five things to pray for. This outline may help you.

One: "That only the righteous would have influence." Speak people's names and proclamations, that they would receive guidance and wisdom and that they would receive the truth.

Prayer: "Lord, if they choose not to rule righteously, I ask that you would take their authority away, turn them down another path." I've seen this work! Here are just a few scriptures to speak.

Isaiah 9:6-7
Isaiah 46:12-13
Psalm 33:5-9
Psalm 77:13-15
Exodus 15:13

And, there are many more besides these. Build your own list and begin to speak them.

Two: "That justice would be restored."

Psalm 7:6-17
Psalm 11:7
Psalm 33:5, 11
Proverbs 29:26
Isaiah 42:1-4
Isaiah 51:4-8

Three: "That evil would be seen for what it is." A person who can tell the difference, has wisdom from God. The one that cannot, is deceived. In the book of Acts chapter two, we see the Lord opening many people's eyes to this, so that they repented of their wickedness when Peter told them to. Also, in Acts 19:13-20, evil was seen for what it was and people brought objects of wickedness, destroying them, repenting and holding the Lord in high honor.

Four: "That the truth would be restored."

John 14:6
John 16:13-15
John 17:17-19
John 18:37

Five:"Pray for Salem".

Salem is Oregon's Capital. So for you, the Lord may choose for you a different city(ies).

It seems like the state capitals that I've been to are less morally inclined than the rest of the state, on average. No wonder, the demons want to influence the leaders.

What every country needs is for its believers to organize to do the work of God.

Question

Question: What is the most difficult situation you have been in?

Answer: I have been in the world's largest battles. They were so big at times that the demons were surrounding me on every side, far beyond the horizon (even above and below me), and they weren't just one deep, either. However, those times were not my most difficult. The Lord helped me prepare for those things. The most difficult situation is keeping my sin nature under control on a daily basis. This will also be your biggest battle.

Paying Attention

Around August 1988, I started to get prophecies for different parts of the world. One day I wrote out several pages of them. Some of them I had already thought about for weeks and some just came as I wrote. I told a group of friends about the prophecies and asked if they would like to read them. There was absolutely no interest. The prophecies contained the Berlin wall coming down, and the order in which the countries recieved their independence from the Soviet Union, flooding in China and other disasters in the South Asia area, a huge earthquake (approximately 9.0 to 9.3) along the Ural Mountains in Russia (this is the only prophecy I can remember that hasn't yet happened) and other things. As the years went by and prophecies happened, still other friends weren't interested in reading them. In the mid 1990's, with most of the prophecies fulfilled, I threw out all the paperwork. There just wasn't any interest. Since then, I haven't written down prophecy like that. Did I grieve the Holy Spirit by throwing the paperwork away, so that he hasn't given me that many at one time again? Or, have I not been paying attention and listening? What motives did my friends have in not wanting to hear the voice of the Lord and read an important historical document? Out of disappointment, I threw it away. Does it take a life that's 97% obedient to Him to write such things down, or 97.1% or??? How close to greatness is your life? When the Holy Spirit is grieved, he almost always silently pulls back, so that we don't know how close to greatness we were.

Did anyone else besides Mike and I see God shake all creation several times in 1992? Not that I am aware of. So, the other more than six billion people missed it. How much are we not seeing due to the deception of the sin nature?

Almost, 100%! Some know so little of him that they say, "Where's God?" It takes all of our strength to do what is right to break the veil of sin/deception/death to see the Light.

NOTES

Jesus is Lord

Chapter Fourteen

Sermon

In the beginning, God created man to live in harmony with Him forever. Man had a choice if he wanted this or not. Man rebelled at God's warning. Corruption entered into all creation including the flesh of man. That corruption of the flesh even stains the soul that has eternal existence since God said, "Let us create man in our image," so both body and soul die. However, God, in his love, did not ask mankind to do what he himself was not willing to do. He sent his son Jesus, "the Word of God made flesh" to fulfill obedience to perfection, since all others had fallen short of perfection. Jesus willingly laid down his life for us. He requested that he be made a curse for us to take away our sins, restoring a right relationship with him. Not only did he receive a brutal beating beyond recognition, he was then spiked to a cross to his last breath. The first thing love is, is commitment. He has done this for us.

Jesus commanded his disciples to stay in Jerusalem until they had been clothed with power from on high. In the book of Acts, chapter two, we see large numbers of people receiving the Holy Spirit, something that had never occurred before. Once we receive the baptism of the Holy Spirit, he dwells within us. Spiritual things are spiritually discerned. No one knows the mind of God except God. We who believe that Jesus is our Lord and Savior are now born again of the Spirit and have open communication with God, as was his original intent. Our connection to him is now reestablished from Adam and Eve's rebellion.

Few decide to fully develop that relationship and some even teach against it. Why? The Lord is glorious, majestic, awesome in wonders, beautiful, trustworthy, eternal, all-knowing, pure, holy, loving, and any attribute toward what can be called good. There is no one and nothing like him. Yet, not everyone knows him. Those who love him will share him. Those who love him will give whatever their means are empowered by the name of Jesus through the Holy Spirit to do good works which he has called us to do. Ephesians 2:10 says, "For we are God's workmanship, created in Christ

Jesus to do good works, which God prepared in advance for us to do." Have total confidence in him. He will provide anything his work requires. When you give up what you have, you get what he has! Send me!

Friday, September 13, 1991, on break time at work, I read a large ad in a newspaper that read, "International Psychic Fair". It would be a three-day event held at the Montgomery Park building in N.W. Portland. When someone gets close to the Lord, many emotions that the Lord has will show up in your thinking. In a very indignant way, I thought, "I don't remember them calling me up and getting permission to hold this in my city!" The Lord wasn't happy, so I wasn't happy. After much coaxing, I talked my friend Bruce into going there and taking care of business. Bruce's wife Cindy and another friend, Laura, would come on this prayer mission. The preparation time in prayer went well. I could visualize many large angels with us. They were a pure holy white with shimmering iridescent green and pink colors where the light would hit if it was just right, as they moved. Bruce's van was surrounded by these angels as we drove from his house in Beaverton. We had some difficulty in finding the building, so we stopped to look around N.W. Portland. In the night, our spiritual eyes could see a column of demons that went into the sky. That must be it! We rounded a city block and could see part of the huge lit sign that said, "Montgomery Park". Upon parking and getting out of the van, I spotted many demons on the outside of the building keeping watch over it, and ready to follow home fair attendees, if they desired. I confidently, with a slight undertone of sarcasm, said, "We're here" to them. The enemy isn't used to seeing someone using their authority given to them by God to go out and set the captives free. The enemy was dumbfounded. I spoke Matt. 18:18 over them and any other demons inside, then released angels on them. Once dominion was well established, it was time to go in. The fair was in a large room with one side all glass, facing the lobby. There were dozens of people performing various kinds of witchcraft. People were coming out of the room with looks of intrigue and deep thought. Demons were influencing the attendees and had already possessed those in charge. There was a woman collecting money as people went in. We agreed that we weren't going to pay to get in a cursed place like that. So, we prayed in the lobby more quietly than usual (as to try and not get too much attention). A few minutes into prayer, we could see the tarot cards not working properly for the lady who was also collecting the money. She began to get frustrated. A few others in the room were also agitated. That's when the four of us decided to walk around the inside of the building and pray for it. We did that on the second story around some offices for about twenty minutes, until a security guard asked what we were up to. We were fortunate to not be asked to leave the building. Once more at the lobby, we spotted another room sharing a wall with the fair. It was a larger room that had a free art exhibit. We slipped in there and found a nearly perfect place to put our hands against the wall to project the power of God right into the psychic fair. Shoved up against the wall were some extra room dividers. Cindy and Laura went elsewhere, while Bruce and I got behind the dividers, almost out of anyone's sight. After asking God what should be prayed, he gave me the book of Amos, starting at chapter two. It describes how the Lord will not turn back his wrath against his enemies. Clearly, God was very incensed about the witchcraft taking place on the other side of the wall. The power of God that went off as we spoke was going off like huge shotgun blasts. There was also lightning and we even threw in a few grenades. Once the work was done, we went back to the lobby to peer into the fair's room. The word of knowledge the Lord gave me about some at the fair becoming ill had come true. The woman receiving money at the door and working tarot cards had looked at ease at the very beginning. As the anointing grew, the tarot cards weren't working properly, and she got frustrated. By the time we were in the lobby for the second time, she looked ill. After the work was complete and we were in the lobby for the third time, she was walking out of the room and looked like she was about to throw up.

Now, the few that came out from attending the psychic fair didn't have curses of divination on them. They no longer had looks of intrigue. Their comments were along the lines of the fair being a waste of money.

Participating in divination has dire consequences that are mostly hidden away from us due to the deception of the sin nature. It's the opposite of a blessing from God. It's death (I've heard that high level witches usually don't live long). Also, there were three "Christians" I recognized coming out of the fair when we first got to the lobby. All three have since had issues. One has now passed away (he was only in his thirties). Having a shorter life is common for those who practice witchcraft.

We decided to leave after observing the satisfactory effects of the Lord's work. We traveled north to visit mutual friends. As we came back south, we crossed the Fremont

Bridge that overlooks the Montgomery building. Our spiritual eyes were still working when we saw that the whole building was holy lit up. The ground around for several blocks was also lit up. On the roof were lookout angels on each corner, with many angels dancing around a large fire in the middle. The dance looked like a cross between a square dance and something tribal African. Instead of death covering those attending, it became a party for angels. How glorious it was to participate! Yet, the thought came to mind, "there are about one million people living in this area, why did only four come to oppose it?" Where are the people who will say, "No" to Satan? Few are taught accurately about such things. Even fewer are skilled enough to deal with these situations. In fact, there are people, discouraging in many ways, these missions that save souls. This is not meant to be! This is why America as a whole is headed in the wrong direction. Even those that don't know the Lord have a sense of future calamity for this country. They are right, but this is preventable. It's the spiritual realm that made the physical, so the spiritual rules everything. Spiritual skill like this saves men's souls, bringing them into the light and out of darkness. There is very little awareness of such things today.

In another mission, (August 8-9, 1992 / 9 p.m.-3 a.m.), I lead a group of seven men. We prayed over a bottle of anointing oil (olive oil) for a mission on Murry Hill. It's a rock quarry that's no longer operating. At the time, it didn't have any development on it like it does today. We were on the south side of Murry Hill making very loud and bold proclamations that night for Mexico, all the way to the tip of South America (but mostly countries south of Mexico to the tip of South America). I threw the bottle of anointing oil south. When it hit the ground, this whole area lit up. More than one continent! This broke a significant amount of demonic powers over this area! Since then, I've been told by many people about how different nations have opened to the gospel, with some in revival. Once the curses were broken, the people could see His light. This prayer affected hundreds of millions of people.

THE SPIRIT OF THE ONE AND ONLY LIVING GOD IS IN ME. HOW COULD THAT NOT POSSIBLY BUT EFFECT ALL CREATION!

For anyone who counts themselves a born again spirit-filled believer in Jesus Christ, count yourself amongst my friends and I who have seen these miracles and many more. But, before I list them, I would like to pay my respects to them. Many of them are now with the Lord, some of them through trials of the enemy. Many were taken at a young age. But, we must continue. The truth burns within us, and we can trust the Lord. He knows best. The Lord has given them a great reward that will last forever and they will never be put to shame.

We have seen, face to face, more than one thousand people make Jesus their Lord and Savior, healings of every imaginable kind including the dead rising back to life, food multiplying, water parting, teleportation, words of wisdom and knowledge, prophecy, ministry that was so effective that it lead to the involvement of all three archangels many times, signs and wonders in the earth, on the earth, and in heaven (outer space), prayers that will last for all generations into eternity.

THE SPIRIT OF THE ONE AND ONLY LIVING GOD, WHO HAS MADE ALL THINGS, IS IN YOU. HOW COULD THIS NOT POSSIBLY BUT EFFECT ALL CREATION!

NOTES

NOTES

Chapter Fifteen

The Future

I've seen people prophesy various things over the years. Some I knew wouldn't come true, some I wasn't sure about, and some I knew would come true.

There is one ingredient that makes prophesying a disaster more tricky than in the Old Testament days where just one person at a time may have had the anointing. It is other spirit-filled believers. If a natural disaster is going to happen and it gets prophesied, then another believer may intercede, asking God to relent. If the Lord stops the disaster, then the person that prophesied looks stupid or like a false prophet. Unless other people find out that someone asked the Lord to relent, then a reputation could be hurt. Upon hearing a prophecy of a disaster that I knew might take place, I asked God for it not to happen and it didn't.

I've had something similar happen to me in the 1990's. The Lord wasn't happy with some sin that was going on in Los Angeles, California (I don't remember what it was). The Lord gave me a prophecy that He was 'going to wash the city into the ocean unless they repented.' I called the Los Angeles Times newspaper and placed an ad with the prophecy. After placing the ad, the customer service representative called me back a few minutes later explaining that the newspaper didn't accept those types of messages. It took some of my time already to figure out how this warning would be made public and now the opportunity was gone. I never did figure out another source to get the word out. The Lord may hold the newspaper responsible for denying His Word a public voice. I said, "Lord, what now?" I did feel some guilt, but I also discharged my responsibility in warning the people as best as I could. Days later as I watched the news, the meaning of 'washed into the ocean' became clear. Some of the heaviest rains in modern history were damaging the city. Some homes were destroyed. Nevertheless, the rains trailed off and didn't do as much damage as the wording in the prophecy suggested. The Lord told me he reduced the damage because many he knew cried out to him for relief.

There is more than enough spirit-filled talent to get exact times and dates of disasters, but it's a little bit more of a complicated world.

After much prayer, here are some answers to future events (written April 2011).

Natural Disasters

Just in the last decade we've seen major increases in catastrophic disaster, both in death of people and monetary damages.

Indonesia quake and tsunami, 2004, hundreds of thousands dead; Haiti earthquake, 2010, hundreds of thousands dead; U.S. hurricane Katrina, 2005, the costliest natural disaster in the history of the country; Japan, March 11, 2011, earthquake 9.0 and called 'a thousand year quake' and devastating tsunami, the costliest natural disaster in human history, also an estimated 25,000 dead.

There is a one hundred percent guarantee these things will continue unless the nations repent of their wicked ways and turn to God. Otherwise Satan will have his way with them.

Financial Disaster

There is a one hundred percent guarantee that there will be more financial upheaval if the nations don't repent and turn from their wicked ways. Otherwise, Satan will have his way with them. When this happens even as it is right now and in the future, don't just point your finger and blame bankers. The system is corrupt because of the wickedness of the people. So, it's an extension of what is in men's hearts.

In 1998, a hedge fund called 'Long Term Capital Management' (LTM for short) leveraged their money too much and their investments went bad. The Federal Reserve of the United States had to get together some big banks to stave off systemic collapse of the world financial system. It took about one billion dollars and a few months to get things back to normal. God was gracious in warning us about too much leverage. Nevertheless, the United States hasn't learned its lesson and now the whole developed world is lusting for more leverage with derivatives than ever before, with about six hundred trillion dollars worth of them, or equal to about fifteen times the gross domestic output of the entire world! Yes, just derivatives. It's a gigantic gambling casino where if one player defaults, everyone around the world could have liabilities beyond what they could pay. So, in 2008, the inevitable happened. The over-borrowing and derivatives market crashed. It was so big compared to 1998 that worldwide intervention was needed! The total bill from this preventable disaster is still continuing. It may have already exceeded five trillion dollars worth of intervention (Yah, five thousand times worse than the last financial disaster, and still counting)!

This ongoing financial disaster may even continue until we have the next 'big one.' My best guess (prayer and research) puts the next 'big one' happening, between 2019 and 2025. Don't take this as an absolute prophecy. It could be sooner or later. At least you have some time to prepare. The Lord gave the world ten years to figure it out between disasters. Will they figure it out before it's too late the next time?

Plague

In the foreseeable future (at least five years) I see no new mass disease spreading worldwide, like the pandemic that killed fifty to one hundred million people from 1917 to 1920.

War

I've gotten little feedback in prayer about his, so I'm not an authority on it.

Future of America

The U.S., as a whole, is turning rapidly away from God. In 1991, I saw a vision of a holy white cloud over the country. It represented God's covering. Such a covering takes decades, if not centuries to build up that level of blessing. By 2000, I saw another vision of that same covering, only this time there were areas of the country that had no covering, and that covering was shrinking! So, when the terrorist attacks of September 11, 2001 happened I was shocked like everyone else, but I wasn't surprised. Unless this nation turns away from its murders, adulteries and thefts, it should expect more of the same. God and sin don't mix. Abortions in most cases are murder. Unmarried people having sex as a commonly accepted practice and parades in cities flaunting homosexuality! God will not be mocked! Eternal damnation is their lot!

When the deception of the sin nature is removed from your body and you slip into eternity, the truth will be totally revealed to you and all will see how right and just God is. In that day, those who didn't love the Truth will go to eternal torment. They will realize too late that I was their only real friend, since all others really hated them by helping them believe lies. The Lord will not ask you to give something up unless He has something better for you.

Chapter Sixteen

Conclusion

My ministry of praying over large areas was never supposed to happen in the current form you've read. If the nations were faithful, there wouldn't be battles like this to fight. But, now I'm like one who was spoken about in the 'parable of the talents,' Matt. 25:14-30. I'm one who was faithful with the five talents of money, and those that decided not to be faithful like the servant that received one talent, had it taken away from him and given to the one that now had ten. The work of the Lord must continue. What they wouldn't do, the Lord has chosen me to do. The unfaithful have given up their faith. I've received it. I've received the power they could've had. My goal is not more power. My goal is to know the Lord, this is where he has sent me.

It's been twenty years since Mass Scale Warfare started. The effects have been good, but not entirely as expected. I thought by clearing out the demons in any area it would bring revival. That wasn't always the case. Some countries did and still are experiencing revival, but the U.S. hasn't. This was a disappointment. The Lord did tell me that it would be worse if it didn't get prayed over. People still have their own free will.

There are some other good effects that include a significant increase in Christian media; books, music, and television. The Lord has given himself a voice in the media; TBN (Trinity Broadcast Network). TBN is now worldwide, amen! Also, spiritual knowledge is more common. I've fought so hard for all these things. There are many anointed teachers out there, not just a few. What's most needed right now is spiritual discipleship and teaching that faith/miracles are normal. Then, the kinds of works you see in this book would be done by many, not just a few as it is now.

His power through me has shaken all creation several times; a feat that no one else will ever do. There was more raw power released in one of those shakings than all the other miracles and human power that will ever be exerted. This shaking is a sign of the Lord's second coming (and a

Jesus is Lord

few other things). If you want to do something great for God, live a pure obedient life. This to God is greater than seeing all creation being shaken.

This shaking was done with His power, I could not save myself, I have no reason to be prideful. The greatest miracle I've seen wasn't one of those times; it's someone passing from death to life by giving their life to the Lord, I have no reason to be prideful. The least in heaven is having a better day than one of those days, I have no reason to be prideful.

Surely there is a God. The Bible says who he is. HE IS EVERYTHING WHO HE SAYS HE IS. Jesus is Lord.

NOTES

NOTES

CPSIA information can be obtained at www.ICGtesting.com
Printed in the USA
LVOW041503130612

285980LV00006B/56/P

9 781613 796955